# SHALL WOMAN PREACH?

## OR

# THE QUESTION ANSWERED

# SHALL WOMAN PREACH?

## OR

# THE QUESTION ANSWERED

BY

## LOUISA MARIAH LAYMAN WOOSLEY

### September 2018

**Memphis (Cordova), Tennessee**

**Cumberland Presbyterian Church**

Published in cooperation by The Historical Foundation of the Cumberland Presbyterian Church and the Cumberland Presbyterian Church in America, The Discipleship Ministry Team of the Ministry Council, and the Communication Ministry Team of the Ministry Council, Cumberland Presbyterian Center, 8207 Traditional Place, Cordova (Memphis), Tennessee, 38016-7414.

This book was originally published by the author in 1891 and reprinted by Frontier Press in 1989 on the anniversary of Louisa Woosley's ordination. The period in which the original manuscript was prepared should be kept in mind when reading this volume. No changes have been made to the original text. Funded, in part, by your contributions to Our United Outreach.

First printing in this format, September 2018.

ISBN-13: 978-1-945929-20-5
ISBN-10: 1-945929-20-0

OUR UNITED OUTREACH
Made Possible In Part By Your Tithe To Our United Outreach

iv

v

In October 1938, a petite gray-haired grandmother stood behind the pulpit of the Marion Cumberland Presbyterian Church and presided over a meeting of Kentucky Synod as moderator. At age seventy-six, she demonstrated the same discipline and skill in leadership that had insured the success of her difficult ministry. Elected to the office of moderator by acclamation, this woman now stood before a synod that had refused to recognize the validity of her ordination in 1889, almost fifty years before. Because of her tenacity of spirit and her deep commitment to God's call, Louisa M. Woosley was unafraid to challenge the tradition of the church that refused to admit women into the clerical office. Her efforts were rewarded as the church reversed its attitude toward her and other women within her lifetime.

*Dr. Mary Lin Hudson*
*Memphis Theological Seminary*

# SHALL WOMAN PREACH?

To

CHRISTIANS

STRIVING FOR A MORE

COMPLETE MASTERY OF THIS QUESTION, AND TO THOSE

EARNESTLY SEEKING THE TRUTH,

IS THIS LITTLE BOOK

*Most Affectionately Dedicated*

BY

L. M. W.

## INTRODUCTION.

——o——

In apearing before the public for the first time as an author, I am not insensible to the criticism to which this little volume may be subjected. I claim no perfection, in either the style or matter of the composition, as I make no pretension to scholarship. My chief aim has been to present biblical truths in such a form that the anxious inquirers after truth may be better able to understand the commands and will of God respecting the much-disputed question of the ordination of women. I have written this little book with an eye single to the fact, that "of making many books there is no end; and much study is a weariness the the flesh."

To avoid being lengthy, I have made my arguments as plain and as pointed as possible, and hope that the reader will lay aside any preconceived notions, and give this investigation an honest hearing. I have confined my remarks exclusively to an investigation of what the English Scriptures teach on this subject. I am willing for an impartial public to test the contents of this volume by the sacred text, without consulting Prof. A., Dr. B., or the law of Mr. C. I know it has been boastfully said, that "women have no right to preach." Lately, however, the times have changed. America now has a hundred women preachers to where she had only one forty years ago, and these women are recognized as preachers by all denominations common among us. Even the Baptists have ordained women to the work of the gospel ministry.

Finally, this little volume is given to the public, with the sincere desire on the part of the author, to promote Bible truths, and to aid others in deciding to help us in the spread of the gospel. My chief design has been to be a guide to those who are earnestly desiring to know the truth on this much-vexed question; to afford a concise, yet comprehensive, Bible argument for the benefit of the mass of common readers; to aid in procuring, if possible, more uniformity of sentiment and practice in the Church to which the author esteems it an honor to belong. I ask the reader to divest himself of all prejudice; to read this little volume carefully and prayerfully, before he comes to the conclusion that it teaches error. Be sure that you can prove by the Word of God that it is wrong. If you cannot disprove the author's position by a "Thus saith the Lord," then have the courage of conviction to embrace all the truth herein taught. And now may the Holy One in Israel, in whose Church there is "neither male nor female," enlighten you, and lead you into all truth, and enable you to "be ready always to give every man that asketh you a reason of the hope that is in you, with meekness and fear."

This little book is sent forth after much prayer, and careful investigation of God's Word, with the hope that it may help all, into whose hands it may fall, to a better understanding of the truth; and that it may be wielded by the great Head of the Church as an instrument for the spread of truth and righteousness.          L.M.W.

CANEYVILLE, KY., April 20th, 1891.

## CONTENTS.

——o——

# OBJECTIONS ANSWERED.

——o——

The objections to woman's preaching and ordination, are very numerous, and as frivolous as numerous. Our object in this chapter is to investigate these objections carefully, and to answer them biblically, and in the light of reason.

1. Some say women ought not to preach, because Paul condemns it (or rather, forbids it). "Let your women keep silence in the churches: for it is not permitted unto them to speak."—I. Cor. 14:34. Well, then, if we are to obey this injunction strictly, and to compel our women to keep silence in the churches, see what follows. We take all the women out of our choirs, and oh! what music we would have with our male voices and our bass singers! But you insist that nothing is said against their singing, but against their speaking. Very well, then, women are not to speak in the church courts at all. If that is what is meant, it does seem that, either we have been dull of comprehension, or very rebellious. In many of our church courts the voice of woman has been heard, and is still being heard. For example, we refer to the General Assembly, which met at Union City, Tenn., May, 1890. In the presence of a large audience, and right in the midst of the transaction of business by that intelligent body, a woman (Mrs. Louisa Ward) was called for. She mounted the rostrum, and we all heard her voice, as she stood for forty minutes defending her own cause. All this was in opposition, too, to what Paul said, as some would have us believe.

If we are to give Paul a literal interpretation, then women may not even pray or talk in church, for they are not permitted to speak. Where then is the authority for their testifying for Christ at all? If those persons, who insist on a literal interpretation of these passages of Scripture, are consistent, and want our confidence, they will never call upon another woman to take part in a praise-meeting: since it is impossible for a woman to praise the Lord, or testify for Jesus, without speaking. Just as long as they allow women to talk in these meetings, we will be constrained to believe they are acting in bad faith: for Paul says they are not permitted to speak, but to be in silence. Then why allow her even to sing? this breaks the silence. It is indeed a good thing to practice what we preach; and if we fail to do so, there is a contradiction. If these objectors want our confidence, they must change either their practice or their preaching. They must

*9*

not allow their women to pray, talk, or even sing in churches: since Paul says "Let your women keep silence."

Has it been the experience of these objectors, that the prayers, songs, and admonitions of godly women, have done them, or the cause of Christ an injury? Who can say he has been harmed by the talk of a good Christian woman? Many, who shall read these pages, have been led to accept Christ through the instrumentality of a woman. Many hearts have overflowed with love, and have swelled with thankfulness to God for her prayers and testimonies. Why then (how can any one object?) object when women speak or pray? Why invite them to come to Christ, or seek salvation at all? since they are forbidden to tell it if the Lord blesses them. It is like inviting them to your house, and then forbidding them to speak to you; or, to your table, and not allowing them to eat; or, like asking a thirsty, way-worn traveler to your well, and then refusing him drink.

If it is a shame for a woman to speak in the church, why ask her to give evidence of a change of heart, or to relate her Christian experience, when she comes forward and asks membership in the church? If a woman were to come forward to join the church, and the pastor should say, Well, my sister, tell us what the Lord has done for you. She makes no reply, and we think it very strange. Then we fancy the preacher says, Do you feel that your sins have been pardoned? She sits like a padlock was upon her mouth. Then he says, Do you want to join the church? And still she sits as mute as a mummy. You say, well there is something wrong; that woman must be crazy. Whereupon Paul rises up and says, oh no; that is all right: "For it is a shame for women to speak in the church."

If this objection is sound, we would better do as we sometimes tell children to do, when they are studying arithmetic, and have their slates covered with figures, and everything is in confusion: we say, rub out and begin anew. So we should get a new charter, and leave the women clear out. If we would understand the meaning of this passage, let us read a little farther. "But they are commanded to be under obedience, as also saith the law. And if they will learn anything, let them ask their husbands at home: for it is a shame for women to speak in the church." The law which Paul mentions, is that which refers to every man's having his own wife, and every woman her own husband (Gen. 3:16): hence the instruction, "Let them ask their husbands at home." But oh! how I do sympathize with the old maids and the widows, for whom Paul makes no provision! And still there is a larger class of women whose husbands do not go to church, and are not religious, that need our sympathy. We can call the roll of a great number within our own knowledge, of women who are our best workers, and the most active in church work; but send them to their husbands for advice or instruction, and what could they learn? What! could Paul have meant that these wives must look to their wicked, and even skeptical husbands to be advised! That would be learning with a vengeance! If she must learn from him at home in silence, why go to church at all?

We are now standing on the threshold of paganism. Between this extreme and heathenism, there is but one more step. We can already feel its chains around us twining, and its hurtful breezes fanning our brows. As we look through the half-open door, we see the wife bow-ing to her husband. The Veda declares she shall have no other god but her husband, or those he delights to worship. Who will step over the line and join hands with heathenism? Who will compel our women to bow to their husbands, and render to them alone complete and strict obedience? If we give Paul a literal interpretation, nothing short of this will answer.

But we will give our objectors all the rope, and admit that it is meant that there are certain times and circumstances when women ought to keep silence—when it would be a shame for them to speak publicly in the church. Cumberland Presbyterians teach, in accordance with the Bible, that the bad are gathered with the good into the Church. "They are not all Israel which are of Israel," and sometimes these give us a great deal of trouble. Being guilty of very grave offenses, such as, dancing, gambling, horse-racing, drinking, and even adultery. These parties must be dealt with, and after complying with certain prescribed rules, if we fail to gain them, we are to tell it to the church. Of course under these circumstnces, it is a shame for a woman to speak in the church. Hence the admonition, "Let all things be done decently and in order." According to Presbyterian polity, a committee may be appointed to see after these matters privately, and so the shame from having such offenses brought before the public, may be avoided, at least to some extent.

The very same record that says, let the women keep silence in the churches, also says let the men (and that too in the very same church) keep silence in the church (see I Cor. 14:28). So according to Paul, there is a time when men should keep silence in the church, as well as the women. But this is a church in confusion, and he admonishes the men to keep silence in such churches; and common sense itself teaches us, that under such circumstances, "It is a shame for women to speak in the church." "For God is not the author of confusion, but of peace, as in all churches of the saints." (verse 33).

It is evident that the scripture referred to in verse 34, applies solely to married women, and it has no reference to religious worship of any kind. If it does, then a woman must sit in church as mute as a mummy. If she even sings she breaks the silence, and thereby be-comes disobedient. God has made no distinction in his kingdom be-tween matron and maid. They all have the same happy privileges. There is no such thing as one gospel for the matron and another for the maid. In the law referred to (Gen. 3:16), "Thy desire shall be to thy husband, and he shall rule over thee," the obedience spoken of has no reference to worship of any kind, and surely not to public meetings, but to the obedience that is due from wife to husband. If worship is meant, the husband is lord over the wife's conscience, and the only one to whom she must give an account. Can he answer for her in judgment? Has she been left out of the covenant of grace? Is she in the world without any sure light to guide her? amenable to no law, human or divine, except that of her husband, to which she must render perfect obedience? Is her husband to be her only teacher, from whom she must learn in silence with all subjection?

. 2. Again Paul says, "But I suffer not a woman to teach, nor to usurp authority, over the man, but to be in silence."—I. Tim. 2:12. With some, this forms a serious objection. They are so afraid that the woman will usurp authority, that they will say she is a usurper, if she undertakes to preach, or even to speak in public. This does not neces-sarily follow. Webster says, usurp means, "To seize and hold in possession by force, or without right." Usurpation then is an illegal seizure, or wrongful possession; and in order to be usurpers, women must take by force, without any right. He who believes that women are usurping authority when they pray or praise God aloud, can be-lieve anything. Woman may preach and not usurp authority. And if she be ordained to the full work of the gospel ministry, she may, if selected by our church courts, preside over their deliberations, and not be a usurper.

The same record says, "But I suffer not a woman to teach." Now we would like for the objector to take this along too; and if he wants even to imitate consistency, let him put his women out of office in the Sunday-school: for they are not allowed to teach. But if they can teach a class of boys in the Sunday-school, why not teach them from the pulpit? If we are always to have a literal interpretation of the Bible, then we insist on having a strict obedience in every case. Also, the objector must not allow women to wear "braided hair, or gold, or pearls, or costly array"—Paul forbids it.—I Tim. 2:9. Who believes that Paul meant to teach us that it is wrong for a woman to wear a gold watch, or a ring set with pearls? Yet this is without doubt the literal meaning of this scripture. "Let not a widow be taken into the number under threescore years old, having been the wife of one man." "But the younger widows refuse."—I. Tim. 5:9-11. Now whoever heard of a church refusing to help a woman because she was a widow? If she is worthy to receive help, and in distress, the Church will assist her regardless of age. But she cannot afford to do so, if we are to obey Paul to the letter. If this scripture requires a literal render-ing, where shall we stop? Why not expect ministers literally to heal the sick, cleanse the lepers, and to cast out devils? They ought to pro-vide neither silver nor gold for their journey. They ought not to salute any man by the way.

Christ, the great Teacher, said, "Whosoever therefore shall confess me before men, him will I confess also before my Father which is heaven."—Matt. 10:32. It is here taught that we ought to confess Christ, but if we give Paul a literal interpretation, then women are prohibited from confessing him: for "Let your women keep silence in the churches." Now in the commonest sort of reason, how can a woman confess Christ before men without breaking this silence? If she does this she becomes a transgressor; yet if she does not confess Christ, he says he will not confess her before his Father in heaven. Poor woman! she stands a bad chance, as transgressors have no part with Christ, and those who will not confess him, he does not own as his children.

Notice that Paul said, "I suffer not a woman to teach, nor to usurp authority over the man." He did not say usurp authority over the Church, but over the man. Is it possible that a woman cannot sing, pray, or teach a Sunday-school class, or preach the gospel, without usurping authority over the man? Have you ever heard of any woman who felt that she was called of God to preach, who tried to force herself upon the Church, or upon the public? Does she try to usurp authority by putting restrictions upon the mouths of men? We are sure that the women are not trying to take the gospel, or any church privileges from the men; neither do they desire to rule over them. Their object is rather to stand by his side—where God intended she should stand—as an helpmeet.

It seems that this subject, as all others, has two extremes. Those who are so bitter against woman's usurping authority, are in danger of becoming usurpers themselves, by passing over the line and going to the other extreme. As a Church, we claim to occupy a medium ground. Then we should not cast the woman down below man, nor raise her up above him. Side by side shall they stand, sharing in the responsibilities of life, and bearing together the heat and burden of the day. Let neither usurp authority over the other, as both are raised from a dead level in sin, to a living perpendicular in Christ. "By strength shall no man prevail."

3. These two passages are the only ones in the Bible that even seem to indicate that a woman shall not preach, while those in the affirmative are very numerous. Some object because there was not a woman among the Twelve. This we admit, but that is no reason why she should not preach, or even be ordained. The objectors ask boastfully, If the Lord intended for women to preach, why were they not represented among the Twelve? If the why is the question, we will right now ask several whys. Why were the twelve patriarchs all men? Why was it that when Jesus ascended the Mount of Transfiguration he took with him only Peter, James and John? Why not take the Twelve and even the seventy? Why was it that when Jesus raised Jairus' daughter, that he suffered only Peter, James, and John to go in to witness the miracle? Canst thou by searching find out God? "Who hath been his counsellor?" "Who hath known the mind of the Lord?" "God moves in a mysterious way His wonders to perform." He works when and where he pleaseth.

Do you say the commission was given to the Twelve? That no women were present, and consequently, woman has no right to ordination? Well then she has no right to a place at the Lord's Supper, because it was instituted with only the Twelve present. Has she no right to commemorate the sufferings and death of her Lord? But the objector says she has, on the ground that she was included in the man, and from the fact that Christ said, "Drink *ye* all of it," and because Paul said, "As often as *ye* eat this bread, and drink this cup, *ye* do show the Lord's death till he come." They will tell us that the women are included in the y-e, ye. Well, then, why are they not included in the broad commission, "Go *ye* therefore, and teach all nations?" It is the very same word in each case—Drink y-e, *ye*, and Go y-e, *ye*. It will be borne in mind that these words fell from the same lips (Christ's), and were spoken to the very same persons. Then can it be possible that he included the men only one time, and the other time, the men and the women? If so, which time did he include the women? Who will say?

These objectors must remember that the Twelve were commissioned by the crucified, dead, buried, and risen Christ, to preach through him as their living head, repentance and remission of sins: in other words, to disciple all nations. In doing this, they preach a risen Savior; for it is the living Christ that saves. We to-day preach him as, "the way, the truth, and the life;" as "the end of the law for righteousness to every one that believeth." But the Twelve were not the first ones commissioned to preach a risen Lord. The world's Redeemer saw fit, in his wisdom, to bestow this honor upon woman. To her he first manifested himself, and spoke words of cheer, quieting her fears, and drying up her tears. When she recognized him, she drew near to worship him, but "Jesus saith unto her, Touch me not; for I am not yet ascended to my Father; but go to my brethren, and say unto them, I ascend unto my Father, and your Father, and to my God, and your God."—Jno. 20:17. "Go tell my brethren that they go into Galilee, and there shall they see me."—Matt. 28:10.

The women returned from the sepulcher, and told these things to the eleven and to all the rest—yea, they departed with great joy, and did run to bring the disciples word. But it is said, "Their words seemed to them as idle tales, and they believed them not." We do not know how many women there were, neither can we give all their names, for they are not revealed. To say the least of it, there could not have been less than five (see Luke 24:10). So "It was Mary Magdalene, and Joanna, and Mary the mother of James, and other women" that were commissioned—that too by Christ himself, and prior to the commissioning of the Twelve. We have no knowledge of any higher authority; and if there is anything in priority of claim, the women have the better right to preach.

4. Yet others object to the ordination of women because there were no women among the seventy disciples. It now becomes necessary for them to prove that there was even one man among them. Upon this point the Bible is silent.

5. Some say, We object because the Confession of Faith has made no provision for the ordination of women. This we frankly admit. And is it not a fact that it has failed to make provision for the

women with regard to the sacrament of the Lord's Supper? Yet they are allowed to surround the sacramental board with the men. Has it made any provision for an elder to sit or act as Moderator in any of our church courts (see p. 85, sec. 17)? But this has been permitted even by the General Assembly.

In the minutes of the General Assembly, which met at Evansville, Ind., 1880, we have the report of the Judiciary Committee on this question (p. 35, report 7) as follows:—"The Judiciary Committee beg leave to report that they have duly considered memorial and reference of Brazos Synod, presenting the question of the eligibility of elders for the position of Moderator in the judicatories of the Church. Your committee are of opinion, and so report, that by the form and genius of our government, there is no discrimination between the ministers and elders constituting our Presbyteries, Synods, and General Assembly, as to powers, duties, and eligibility to office in said courts. Such a discrimination would be disparaging to one-half of said bodies, and destroy that equality in dignity and power, which was intended to exist. To produce this effect would require some express provision. The omission of such provision, your committee considers almost conclusive, that none such was intended. The long existing usage, which will perhaps continue, of selecting ministers to moderatorship is very different from the question of legal eligibility. Your committee are therefore of opinion, and so report, that it is the right of judicatory to elect any member of their body, either minister, or elder, to preside over their deliberations, and that every member is equally eligible, whether he be a minister or elder."—R. L. Caruthers, Ch'm.

This report was concurred in: which thing of itself shows that the General Assembly is not willing to be governed by the silence of the Confession of Faith. It is silent on the baptism of women, and on a great many other things that we practice. If we are to be governed by the silence of the Confession of Faith, then elders are not to preside over our church courts; women must not preach, or even pray in public; they must not partake of the sacrament of the Lord's Supper, and even be refused the sacrament of baptism; she must not teach in the Sunday-school, nor go as a missionary to the heathen lands: for upon all these points the Confession is as silent as death. Who can believe that the compilers of this book ever thought of such a thing as the Church's being governed by its silence? Who will plead for such a course?

By such an admission, and by the fickleness of some; we are reminded of the fable of the hawk and the bat. All these objectors occupy the same position; they have no sure foundation, and are just floating about. If one of their puny arguments fails them, they resort to something else. They are like the bat when caught by the hawk. The hawk says: "You sweet little bird, I'm going to eat you." "Oh, no," says the bat; "you would not eat me! for I'm a mouse." "Well then," says the hawk, "I will let you go; for I ate a mouse a few days ago, and it made me so sick, I don't care about having another vomit." So the little bat flew away very happy, because the hawk had been so clever as to let him go. Another day a cat caught him when she was in search of food, and as she walked off with her prey, she said, "What a nice mouse I have for dinner." "Oh no," says the bat; "you would not eat me! I'm no mouse; I'm only a little bird." And he flapped his wings. "Well then," said the cat, "I'll let you go: for only the other day I ate a bird, and I became choked on the feathers, and I nearly died." And again the little bat flew away, hardly knowing whether he was a bat, a mouse, or a bird.

These objectors would sometimes have us believe that they are birds of the finest plumage, but when they are about to be used up, their "feathers fall," and they would feign themselves to be mice, and begin to beg the question; and like the bat fly away. In reality, they are neither birds nor mice—only bats flying around in the dark, because the light hurts their eyes.

6. Again, others object because there are no instances recorded in the Bible of a woman's being ordained, and they say, there is no scripture in favor of such a course. In a sense, we will admit this. But when they say, Show us when and where any woman was ever ordained, we can ask with as much propriety, when and by whom were Luke, Mark, Apollos, Titus, and Aquila ordained? If they can answer, may we not tell when Mary, Priscilla, Junia, Tryphena, Tryphosa, and Phebe were ordained? No man can show us these things; but they still say, Show us the scripture for ordaining a woman. Well, let them show us the scripture for licensing men, and we can tell them where to find the last named. Begin and carefully read your Bible, and when you come to where it says license men to preach, mark the place: then read on—the next verse says ordain women. In truth, it is a fact, there is no scripture for licensing men; yet it is common, and nothing is said about it. Why this unfairness and inconsistency? Show your scripture for permitting women to

partake of the Lord's Supper, and when this is done, you will be able to prove that women have a right to ordination.

7. Another objection (they say) is, Woman cannot fulfill the commission. She may preach, but she cannot baptize; that is, immerse. This objection deserves only a passing notice, since our Confession of Faith does not say immerse (any more than it says ordain a woman); yet our Church practices immersion, notwithstanding our Confession says, that baptism is rightly administered by pouring or sprinkling water upon the person (see p. 55, sec. 101). This mentions only pouring and sprinkling, yet we claim that it recognizes immersion as baptism: but oh, how silently does it teach it! and yet we practice it. Now in the light of reason, can we not with as much propriety (according to the Conf. of Faith), ordain women as we can baptize by immersion? Is it not as much in sympathy with the ordination of women, as with elders, who preside over our church courts?

8. Again, some say, We believe woman has a right to preach, but not to ordination. They say, Endorse her as an evangelist, and let her go. Well, that is one way of "whipping the Devil around the stump." We would like to see a "thus saith the Lord" for such a procedure. The Cumberland Presbyterian Church has no law for such a course. The Confession of Faith does not say, endorse a woman as a lay evangelist. (We quote Conf. of Faith, page 83, sec. 9-14 under Constitution):

"MINISTERS OF THE WORD.

"9. The office of the ministry is the first in the Church, both for dignity and usefulness. The person who fills it has, in the Scriptures, different titles, expressive of his various duties. As he has the oversight of the flock of Christ, he is termed bishop; as he feeds them with spiritual food, he is termed pastor; as he serves Christ in his Church, he is termed minister; as it is his duty to be grave and prudent, and an example to the flock, and to govern well in the house and kingdom of Christ, he is termed presbyter or elder; as he is the messenger of God, he is termed angel of the Church; as he is sent to declare the will of God to sinners, and to beseech them to be reconciled to God through Christ, he is termed ambassador; as he bears the glad tidings of salvation from place to place, without having his labors confined to any particular church or locality, he is termed evangelist; as he stands to proclaim the gospel, he is termed preacher; as he expounds the word, and by sound doctrine both exhorts and convinces, he is termed teacher; and as he dispenses the manifold grace of God, and the ordinances instituted by Christ, he is termed steward of the mysteries of God. These titles do not indicate different grades of office, but all describe one and the same office,

"10. He that fills this office should possess a competency of human learning, and be blameless in life, sound in the faith, and apt to teach; he should exhibit sobriety and holiness of conversation becoming the gospel; he should rule his own house well, and should have a good report of those who are without.

"11. As the Lord was given different gifts to the ministers of the Word, and has committed to them various works to execute, the Church is authorized to call and appoint them to labor as pastors, teachers, and evangelists, and in such other work as may be needful to the Church, according to the gifts in which they excel.

"12. When a minister is called to take charge of a particular church, it belongs to his office to pray for and with his flock, as the mouth of the people unto God; to feed the flock by reading, expounding, and preaching the Word; to direct the people in singing the praises of God; to administer the sacraments; to bless the people from God; to catechise the children and youth; to encourage Sabbath-school work; to visit officially the people, devoting especial attention to the poor, the sick, the afflicted, and the dying; and, with the ruling elders, to exercise the power of government.

"13. When a minister is appointed to be a teacher in a school of divinity, or to give instructions in the doctrines and duties of religion to youth assembled in a college or university, it appertains to his office to take a pastoral oversight of those committed to his charge, and be diligent in sowing the seed of the Word, and gathering the fruit thereof, as one who watches for souls.

"14. When a minister is appointed to the work of an evangelist, he is commissioned to preach the Word, administer the sacraments, organize particular churches in foreign countries, frontier settlements, or in the destitute parts of the Church, and to establish Sabbath-schools, as wisdom may direct."

According to Dr. Buck, an evangelist is clothed with official authority.

9. Again, others say woman may preach, but she ought not to be ordained, for fear the Church may get some worthless women, and some may come in with impure motives. They will even say, We cannot say anything against the action of the Nolin Presbytery, and then add, We might get a bad one next time, or one that could not do

any good: so we would better stop at this. Well, then, if that is our charter, and we are going to act accordingly, the Church, the ministry, and all will soon die, and the sooner the better. If we are governed according to this principle, on the same ground we must not license and ordain any more men: for if we do, we will be sure to get some vile men with impure motives. Also, we must close and bar the doors of our churches: for if we fail to do this, we will certainly be troubled by some bad members.

10. Yet others object because they say the babies and the little children get sick sometimes, and that would hinder woman as a preacher. Just as though men's children never get sick, and they are never hindered in that respect. And along the same line, others protest on account of child-bearing and nursing, saying that if it were common to ordain women, they would be sometimes elected to attend church courts, and could not, for the above-named reason. We cannot say but it might sometimes so happen, and the women would have to stay at home; but that would be nothing new—it would only be one representative out. Men have stayed at home time and again for the very same reason—afraid to leave their wives even long enough to attend the presbyterial meetings.

11. Some others say, If women are ordained they will necessarily have to travel alone, and in so doing, they will be exposed and disgraced; they will not be looked upon as being respectable. So, brethren, we cannot understand this. We must confess that we are puzzled, and at a loss to know how it is then that the women of our missionary societies, and our Sunday-school conventions, and temperance associations, are not disgraced. How is it that the good women that have crossed the broad waters, and have toiled so faithfully and labored so bravely, still maintain their respectability? We can see no difference in the dangers to which these women are all exposed. The difference is in their engagements. If we are unwilling that our women be exposed by traveling alone, and by speaking in public, we must dissolve our missionary societies, and call our women home from the foreign field. But our objectors say, We cannot do that, because that would stop our work among the heathen, that would be a hinderance to the cause of Christ: for men have not access to the women of heathen lands. And, like David, we will put the women in the front of the battle, and when the war is over, and the victory is won, and the heathen, through the influence of these women, are civilized and christianized; then we men will go over

there and tell them, "It is a shame for women to speak in the church:" we will organize a church, and baptize those converts made through the instrumentality of women.

The commission is, "Go ye, therefore, and teach [or disciple] all nations." These women are doubtless teaching (discipling) these heathen to the best of their ability. The truth is, that human nature is the same everywhere. The plan of salvation never changes. If woman has a right to teach (disciple) the heathen, she has a right to teach at home. And if she has a right to teach (preach, disciple), she has a right to recognition. The Church, in ordaining men, simply recognizes what she believes God has done. Hence, she inquires into their union with Christ, and into the dealings of God with them. If they give satisfactory evidence of being called to the ministry, and of an aptness to teach, she lays hands on them and ordains them. Any man, after showing himself competent to the work of the ministry—not because the Church believes he is called of God, or because of his aptness to teach—is ordained; but because he supports a mustache, or wears men's clothing. The women are coming with the very same story, and knocking at the doors of the various denominations for admittance. They say, this subject is a flame in our hearts, and a fire is kindled in our bones. But a voice from within says, Depart, I know you not, ye poor, cursed women. You can't get in here, because your hair is long, and your features are fine. You are not masculine enough.

12. Well, you say, I don't believe that God calls women to preach. When men of the ministry take this position, they place themselves right by the side of those who say, None are called to preach; and they must take sides with those who deny the operation of the Holy Spirit, even in renewing and regenerating the heart. This is something that we cannot prove by mortal man; but one thing we know, "that the gifts and calling of God are without repentance." "Whatsoever God doeth, it shall be forever: nothing can be put to it, nor anything taken from it: and God doeth it that men should fear before him."

When an opportunity is given by the Cumberland Presbyterian Church for the reception of members, we say to the audience that we receive members by experience, by recommendation, and by letter. They come, men and women. The men give evidence of a change of heart, and are received. The women give evidence of the same; they say, We know in whom we have believed, and His Spirit beareth witness with ours; and they are received. Why? Because the session believes what they say. On this ground the writer was received into the Macedonian congregation of the Cumberland Presbyterian Church. Just so, your presbytery meets, and gives an opportunity to those who wish to become candidates for the ministry, to come forward. They come, men and women. The men tell how God has called them to the holy work of the gospel ministry, and that after a great struggle they have decided to go and preach the best they can. The presbytery receives them under her care. The women say, that they feel that they are called of God (constrained) to preach. The presbytery asks them, How do you know it? They say, Just as we know that our sins have been pardoned. Will you receive us? On this very ground the writer was received as a candidate for the ministry under the care of the Nolin Presbytery. But the objector comes up and says, You did wrong: God does not call women to preach.

Now, if women are worthy of confidence at all, it does seem that they are just as worthy of it in the one case as in the other. And if she can be believed in the former, why not in the latter? If she cannot be trusted in the one, why in the other? So far as the writer is concerned, she would just as soon have those objectors tell her that she is mistaken—her sins have not been pardoned, and that she knows nothing about being born again. And they could just as easily take the Bible, and prove to her that she has no hope of heaven—no title to the inheritance of the saints in light—as they could convince or prove to her, that the Spirit had not said unto her, "Go thou and preach the kingdom of God." When she must doubt one, she will certainly give up the other.

To complete the picture, let us examine some parables of the great Teacher:

"The kingdom of heaven is like unto a net, that was cast into the sea, and gathered of every kind: which, when it was full, they drew to the shore, and sat down, and gathered the good into vessels, but cast the bad away."—Matt. 13:47, 48. Then we have the moral, "So shall it be at the end of the world." We all certainly recognize this picture, and agree that the net is the gospel net: the sea is the world; the good are the righteous; the bad are the unrighteous; the shore is the shore of eternity. In the end, the good (the wheat), or the righteous, shall be safely housed in heaven; while the bad (the tares), or the unrighteous, shall be burned with fire. Again, "The kingdom of heaven is like to a grain of mustard seed, which a man [not a woman] took, and sowed in his field.'' When this gospel net is used by men, or when the gospel is preached by men, it is like the seed planted in the field, "which, indeed, is the least of all seed: but when it is grown, it is the greatest among herbs, and becometh a tree, so that the birds of the air come and lodge in the branches thereof."—Matt. 13:31, 32. We do not wonder that Christ said, "Fear not; . . . thou shalt catch men.'' Then, "as a nail in a sure place, fastened by the master of assemblies,'' he said, "The kingdom of heaven is like unto leaven, which a woman [not a man] took, and hid in three measures of meal, till the whole was leavened."—Matt. 13:33. Then the gospel net in the hands of women, as preachers of the gospel of the kingdom, is to have the effect of leaven upon those that hear and believe their word. "Purge out, therefore, the old leaven, that we may be a new lump. ṁ So we are no more twain, but one. "What, therefore, God hath joined together, let not man put asunder.'' "If this work be of men it will come to naught; but if it be of God, ye cannot overthrow it.'' Then let us beware lest we be found to fight against God.

13. But, after all this, another objector comes along, and says that a woman is not strong enough; her general make-up forbids it; she is too weak physically and intellectually. Well, then, the Bible is on her side; for "God hath chosen the weak things of the world to confound the things which are mighty." The potter hath the power over the clay. It is a fact that this country has over eighty thousand ministers, and the majority of them came from poor, illiterate, and uncultivated families. "Not many wise men after the flesh, not many mighty, not many noble, are called." These all have to learn that it is, "Not by might nor by power, but by my Spirit, saith the Lord." Concerning her intellect, she has so far proved herself adequate to everything she has yet undertaken. Then we are instructed if we lack wisdom to ask of God.

14. But say these doubting Thomases, We cannot believe that woman ought to preach and be ordained, because God said, "Thy desire shall be unto thy husband, and he shall rule over thee," and Paul advised that "The younger women marry, bear children, guide the house, give none occasion to the adversary to speak reproachfully."—I Tim. 5:14. They will say that this is her God-given place in the world and in the Church. This ought not to hinder those who feel that they are called of God to preach his gospel, and it is no reason why the Church should interfere. If we must take this scripture literally, then, Is the Church not under obligation to see to it that

every man earns his bread by the sweat of his face? They forget that even in that sorrowful time the promise of deliverance was given to the woman. All men are not called to preach, neither are all women. The apostle understood this, and that they might be left without excuse, he gave instructions to all. If we are going to follow the instructions of Paul literally, then we will have a Sunday-school for men only, and bass singers only in our choirs, and we'll greet all the brethren with "an holy kiss," while the women stay at home to guide the house.

Paul says, "Art thou loosed from a wife? seek not a wife."—I Cor. 7:27. We wonder if all our objectors will insist on the literal rendering of this passage. We dare say some of them would go to "the jumping-off place," before they would agree to this. It is evident that some have been scratching their tickets, and taking therefrom what did not suit their pet theories. In the same way, we can show from the Bible that there is no God, but after so doing, we would have only what is in the fool's heart. If the men are not to marry, each sex will live independent of the other. The men will run their own affairs, and the women theirs. Neither is to give assistance to the other. So we would have two machines running instead of one. Being separated from the women, the men would be in a dreadful dilemma, and would have no Savior. "But when the fullness of the time was come, God sent forth his Son, made of a woman [not of a man], made under the law, to redeem them that were under the law, that we might receive the adoption of sons"—Gal. 4:4, 5. "There appeared a great wonder in heaven; a woman clothed with the sun, and the moon under her feet, and upon her head a crown of twelve stars; and she being with child cried, travailing in birth."—Rev. 12:1, 2. "And she brought forth her first-born son, and wrapped him in swaddling clothes, and laid him in a manger."—Luke 2:7. Now, through the woman the men can say with us, "Unto us a child is born, unto us a son is given."

Strange, but true, the conception of Christ was first made known to a woman: his coming, or incarnation, was told to a woman: to a woman he first revealed the fact (and she was a poor cast-down woman), that "God is a Spirit; and they that worship him must worship in spirit and in truth." A woman was last at the cross, and first at the tomb. It was to the women he first appeared, and they were the first to hear his words after his passion. They were the first commissioned by their Lord to preach a risen Christ. But if it be true that women are to stay at home and guide the house, and this is her God-given place in the Church and in the world, then her position is the same in both. Then there are no privileges granted to a woman in Christ above those granted to a woman of the world. Then it follows that woman's condition is not bettered by reason of her faith in Christ and her relation to him. How then is a woman profited by the coming of Christ, or by the preaching of the gospel?

15. Others object because the Bible speaks of women who were false prophets, and who did a great deal of harm. Indeed it does seem that the objectors have been driven to despair, and like a drowning man, they have caught at a straw, or something that can give no assistance. There cannot be a counterfeit without the existence of the genuine.

16. Again, the objector will say, We ought to obey strictly the commands of Christ, and we should go so far, and no farther. They say that he did not command women to preach; therefore they have no such right. In so many words, He did not: for there is no specific command to this effect. Neither did he command us to keep Sunday instead of Saturday for the Sabbath: but we do this without any specific command. This change was man's work, not God's. Though there is no command for the ordination of women, their labors in the ministry have been abundantly blessed of God. He sanctions their work, and the Church is not above her Lord. Can she not afford to do as much?

Many other objections might be mentioned, but we deem it unnecessary. All who take the negative of this question, finally take refuge in their strongholds, "Let your women keep silence in the churches," and "I suffer not a woman to teach, nor to usurp authority over the man." All of these allow women to speak on financial questions—and that, too, publicly in the church, if they think more money will be the result. If she succeeds in getting a good collection, they commend her highly, and just so long as she can get a dollar, she is welcome to the floor. Why this thusness? Who will explain?

## *WOMAN.*

——o——

One Rosy morn that opened earth's primal year,
    God sat upon His throne of golden rays;
He viewed His realm of thronging silver spheres,
    And heard them hymning their Creator's praise.
The new-born world was floating 'neath His throne,
    Endowed with all His fullness—Eden blessed;
His noblest work the scepter swayed alone,
    Man formed of God, His image self-expressed.

It was all "good." Infinity was filled
    All glorious, around, beneath, above;
A universe the Master Workman willed
    And wrought of wisdom, beauty, grace, and love.
Where would a hue adorn the lily's bloom?
    What melody the wild bird's song amend?
What aroma enhance the flower's perfume?
    What other good now with earth's fullness blend?

Yet God resolved to better what was good,
    And touch perfection with a grace supreme,
So crowned creation with fair womanhood,
    Gave her to earth to bless it and redeem.
Last from His hand, transcending all He gave,
    God's love and goodness in earth's beauty dressed:
Last near His cross, the first to find His grave;
    Mother, man's first love—wife, his last and best.

—[*Lu B. Clark.*

## WOMAN IN THE GARDEN.

——o——

"And the Lord God said, It is not good that the man should be alone."—Gen. 2:18.

Now let us candidly ask, why not? and whether there be any limit to this statement, as some would have us believe; and if there is, who will have the boldness to draw the line? Is it possible that in one vocation of life it is not good for man to be alone, and in another it is? Then, "Who by searching can find out God," and say whether it is better to be without woman in the physical or spiritual point of view? Is it here taught that it is not good for man to be alone, from the fact that woman is needed at home to administer to the temporal wants of her household, while the man administers to the spiritual wants of others? These are grave questions, and they lie at the root of the matter. "I know that whatsoever God doeth, it shall be forever: nothing can be put to it, nor anything taken from it: and God doeth it, that men should fear before him."—Ecc. 3:14.

We learn that "God created the heaven and the earth," and "all things therein," and when his work was finished, he said, "it was very good." This work included the creation of man. God, the maker of our bodies and the Father of our spirits, designed the happiness of man from the beginning, and created him in his own image. He placed him in the garden, and as a test of his obedience, said unto him, "Of every tree of the garden thou mayest freely eat: but of the tree of the knowledge of good and evil thou shalt not eat of it."—Gen. 2:16, 17. The penalty annexed for violation of this command was death—the strongest motive possible to secure man's obedience.

Soon after the giving of the law, "God said, it is not good for the man to be alone;" and he caused a deep sleep to fall upon the man, and proceeded to take one of his ribs and make woman. We are here taught a very important lesson; for this is God who "spake and it was done; he commanded and it stood fast." He by his power could have spoken the woman into existence, but in his wisdom he designed to show us the relation the one sustains to the other, and that each should share alike the responsibilities of life. Mark, will you, there were not two laws given, neither were there two promises made. The law was given before the formation of the woman and never repeated; yet the woman understood that while they kept that law she with her husband was happy in holding communion with God.—Gen. 3:1-3. She, as well as he, was held responsible for partaking of the forbidden fruit; for we learn that the eyes of both of them were opened, and when they knew what they had done they hid themselves from the presence of the Lord.—Gen. 3:7, 8. Shame covers their faces; anguish fills their hearts; justice cries for their blood; a cloud of darkness, like that of death, overspreads the sky: man is doomed to die.

"I was in the Spirit on the Lord's day, and heard behind me a great voice, as of a trumpet, saying, I am Alpha and Omega, the first and the last: and what thou seest write in a book."—Rev. 1:10, 11. "And there appeared a great wonder in heaven; a woman clothed with the sun, and the moon under her feet, and upon her head a crown of twelve stars: and she being great with child, cried, travailing in birth, and pained to be delivered."—Rev. 12:1, 2. This is the fulfillment of the promise made to the woman in the garden of Eden: and "When the fullness of the time was come, God sent forth his Son made of a woman, made under the law, to redeem them that were under the law, that we might receive the adoption of sons" (Gal. 4:4, 5), through the seed of the woman wearing "the crown of twelve stars." The twelve stars point us to the fact that men and women under the patriarchal and apostolic dispensations were made one in Christ.

Woman was given to man not as a slave, not as an inferior, not as a superior, but as an helpmeet. Nothing is said of man's having authority over the woman; neither is it said that the man should have dominion over the things of earth to the exclusion of the woman. To them (and not to him) did God say, "Be fruitful, and multiply and replenish the earth, and subdue it; and have dominion over the fish of the sea and over the fowls of the air, and over every living thing that moveth upon the earth."—Gen. 1:28. In this holy state God gave this happy pair the world as an inheritance. Not a word is said of man's sphere and woman's sphere, neither of his authority and her subjection; so, without a doubt, they stood on equal footing under the law. "And the Lord God caused a deep sleep to fall upon Adam, and he slept; and he took one of his ribs, and closed up the flesh instead thereof." Of this rib he made a woman. God certainly made no mistake here. If he intended for woman to be man's inferior, we think it reasonable to suppose he would have taken a bone out of man's foot, instead of taking a rib from near his heart. Then all would have understood that she was inferior to man. And had God designed she should be man's superior, possibly he would have taken a bone above his heart, perhaps from his head. This of itself would have been a declaration of her superiority. But she was made of man's rib, and coming from near his heart, is his equal, and his helpmeet.

We will consider woman as a helpmeet in presenting the world with the Star of Hope, the Sun of Righteousness, the Babe of Bethlehem, the Man of Sorrows, the King of Kings, the Wonderful Counsellor, the Mighty God, the Everlasting Father, the Prince of Peace. Woman, it is readily seen, is an important factor in the beginning and completion of the world's redemption, and of the final glorification of any soul. The last victory gained, as well as the first, shall be through the seed of the woman, which is to bruise the serpent's head. But shall we here draw the line and say she shall proceed no further.?

God has ever honored the fair sex. The name of Mary has become immortal by reason of the saying, "The Holy Ghost shall come upon thee, and the power of the highest shall overshadow thee: therefore also that holy thing which shall be born of thee shall be called the Son of God."—Luke 1:35. Truly she was a helpmeet in presenting the world with an infant Savior, through the only source from which deliverance could come. She was worthy of giving birth to the Savior, but not worthy to proclaim his salvation, as some would have us believe.

Some say there was a change after the fall, and this we also believe. Then it was said the man should rule over the woman (Gen. 3:16), but is it not just as true that through the seed of the woman both the man and the woman gain what was lost? Are they not by faith restored and made one in Christ? Is not mankind by grace raised up to the standard of perfection laid down in the law? Man, having become a fallen being, would according to his own evil nature rule over his wife, although she still loved him. This we know from observation. How often is it the case, that man in a state of nature, in his sins and away from God, is very brutal in his treatment toward his wife! Often nothing but the laws of our commonwealth restrain him. But when he is "born of God," and made a partaker of his divine nature, then there is a change brought about; he respects and honors his wife, knowing that in Christ there is neither "male nor female." To test the truth of this statement, let us contrast Pagan and Christian womanhood. Woman's position to-day in society is very different from what it was in former ages. This is admitted by all. The change in the last century, or even in the last fifty years, is very marked. Is this change for the better, or for the worse? This is an important question.

The women of to-day are preparing themselves for almost every vocation: you find them at the counter, in the clerk's office, in the school-room, in the post-office, in the practice of medicine and law, among poets and inventors; and in some parts of the United States, they are holding civil office. Also we find some of them among editors and preachers. All this means something. This is an age of improvement, and this is certainly an indication of something greater to follow. But is it for the best that woman come to the front and take her stand for God and truth; or will it impede the progress of the cause of Christ? Is it right for woman to preach? This question is agitating the religious public to-day, and must be settled one way or the other. The number of women in the ministry has been doubled and trebled in the last few years. According to the best statistics there are now in the United States nearly eight hundred lady preachers, and this does not include the Sunday-school workers and the women of various branches of the missionary cause. Are these women out of their places? are they making the world worse? are they forbidden by the Bible to preach? If so, then they ought to be prohibited by the Church from preaching. They should not have the sympathy of the Christian world, neither should they be acknowledged as ministers, nor allowed to occupy the pulpit. But if the Scriptures sanction woman's preaching, she has a right to ordination, and to the same assistance and recognition as men.

The opinion of men is not what we want now. They have not settled, and can not settle this question. But we want a "Thus saith the Lord," as it is given us in the book of inspiration; and this we must obey. No one can gainsay this. Woman was the agent through whom Satan brought sin and death into the world, but God told her that she should be the agent through whom he would work to sin's destruction, and to the abolition of death. That is, from her seed should come the Deliverer, who should bring redemption and deliverance from death. Still, in consequence of sin, and in her fallen condition, she should be subject to lordship and cruelty. She had the promise through her seed (that is Christ) that she should, under the gospel of Christ, be restored to her original condition. She and her husband were to enjoy the same privileges; she should be subject to her husband in the same sense in which the Church is subject to Christ. "Therefore shall a man leave his father and mother and cleave unto his wife and they twain shall be one flesh."—Gen. 2:24. And if one, then there can be but one law by which they are to be governed. "But I would have you know, that the head of every man is Christ; and the head of the woman is the man: and the head of Christ is God."—I Cor. 11:3. Therefore, as the Church is subject unto Christ, so let the wives be in subjection to their own husbands in everything. The union between the man and the woman being of the same nature as that between the Church and Christ, she is to render obedience to her husband just as the Church is obedient to Christ, and the husbands are to love their wives, as Christ also loves the Church. From this we understand that, as Christ rules or watches over the Church in love, so the husband is to rule or watch over the woman in love; and as the Church is in love obedient to Christ, so the woman in love should be obedient to her husband. "Likewise, ye wives, be in subjection to your own husbands." "Likewise, ye husbands, giving honor unto the wife, as unto the weaker vessel, as being heirs together of life; that your prayers be not hindered."—I Pet. 3:7. It is manifest that God intended the two should have the same care the one for the other, and the dominion of the man over the woman, he being the head of the family, was to be of such a nature, as to give honor to the woman, as being the "weaker vessel," not as the weaker person. Now a vessel is that which contains something. Woman is physically, not mentally or spiritually, weak. Seeing that we are heirs together of life, "we have this treasure in earthen vessels." Then, lest "our prayers be hindered," let the man and the woman stand side by side, shoulder to shoulder, in defense of the cause of Christ. It necessarily follows, if they are heirs together of the grace of life, that each has a share (an equal share) in all that pertains to salvation through Christ; for the woman was created in the image of God just as was the man. And if she gains anything in Christ she gains equally as much as the man. God created them in his own image, "male and female created he them; and blessed them and called their name Adam" (Gen. 5:2); but Adam called his wife's name Eve (Gen. 3:20). They were pronounced good; there was nothing wanting. The divine law was their guide, and having rebelled they were sent out of the garden, and a flaming sword which turned every way and kept the way of the tree of life was placed at the gate.

Through Christ the sword is turned aside, the door is open; and they entering by faith are made partakers of his divine nature, and are one in him, and together they are to conquer the foe and to trample Satan under their feet. This view is plain, straightforward and tenable, and as we shall see further is the only one that will not cause the Bible to contradict itself.

So we will notice carefully these oft-repeated and misapplied passages of scripture; remembering that a truth uttered once, remains a truth forever. In order to get a clear knowledge of the seeming prohibitions and restrictions, as are left upon record by Paul, and of the privileges and rights allowed women, we must bear in mind that the obedience rendered was to be to her husband ("he shall rule over thee"). "But I suffer not a woman to teach, but to be in silence." [Reason for—] "For Adam was first formed, then Eve." To a soul earnestly seeking the truth, this scripture is not hard of comprehension. Yet these passages are relied on above all others to prove that women ought not to preach or speak in public. The phrase here, "your women," of course, has reference only to the married women; and learners and teachers are two different things. It is evident that they were not then trying to instruct by preaching, but rather trying to learn by asking questions, and of course it was not a suitable time to ask questions. The apostle did not say if you would teach or preach, to teach or preach to their husbands at home; but if they (the women) would learn anything, let them ask their husbands at home. The idea that they were teaching cannot be entertained for a moment by any one who studies the language of the apostle. Are learners, teachers? does "learn anything," mean teach anything? or is it wrong only for those who have husbands to speak in the church? if so, I hope our young women will take warning. Paul said nothing to hinder the unmarried from speaking in the church. Is it possible that marriage disqualifies a woman for her religious duties? "And no man taketh this honor unto himself, but he that is called of God, as was Aaron."

We come now to consider the second link in the chain, that is God's dealings with the human family, remembering that "There is no respect of persons with God," and that we are his battle-ax and that he designs through human instrumentality to save the perishing of earth. It is said the gift of God is eternal life. The Holy Spirit, too, is a gift—"How much more will he give the Holy Spirit to them that ask him." And he gives to us the Spirit without measure; but it must be remembered that the gift of the Spirit is one thing, and the gifts of the Spirit is another, and quite a different thing. We may have the Spirit, but not have the gifts of the Spirit. We may be gifted in that we have all the advantages that wealth and education can give, and yet fail, because we are not gifted of God. We are admonished to "try the spirits whether they be of God," and we believe that the women are as capable of doing this as the men; hence their accountability. Are they not as capable of receiving the impressions of the Holy Spirit upon their minds and hearts as the men? For this reason we are not willing to attribute all their manifestations of joy to the emotions of nature, and their desires to engage in the cause of Christ to a delusion of the Devil; since "every good gift and every perfect gift is from above." Who art thou, O man, that judgest? Doest thou not the same things? Hast thou, O man, all the embodiment of spiritual wisdom? Can not a woman as well as a man learn that "that the fear of the Lord is the beginning of wisdom?" The Lord grant us understanding.

"Now concerning spiritual gifts, brethren, I would not have you ignorant." "Now there are diversities of gifts, but the same Spirit." "But the manifestation of the Spirit is given to every man to profit withal. For to one is given by the Spirit the word of wisdom, to another the word of knowledge by the same Spirit."—I. Cor. 12:1, 4, 18. So we see the gifts of the Spirit are many. But all these worketh that one and self-same Spirit, dividing to every man severally as he will." "For by one Spirit we are all baptized into Christ's body . . . and we are all made to drink into one Spirit." "For as many of you as have been baptized into Christ have put on Christ. There is neither Jew nor Greek, there is neither bond nor free, there is neither male nor female: for ye are all one in Christ."

God bestows gifts without respect to sex. The body is one and hath many members, "and all members have not the same office." "But now hath God set the members, every one of them, in the body, as it hath pleased him;" and who will dare say unto him, What doest thou? God never intended that there should be any schism in the body, but that the members should have the same care the one for another, and he never intended that one sex should lord it over the other. "And God hath set some in the Church, first apostles, secondly prophets, thirdly teachers." There are gifts many; but have all the same gifts? Paul's instructions to the Corinthian Church was, "Covet earnestly the best gifts," and there is nothing said against women's desiring or coveting these gifts. If God bestows them, has she not a right to improve them? Who will say she shall bury her talent (gift)? "Forasmuch then as ye are zealous of spiritual gifts, seek that ye may excel to the edifying of the Church." God seeks in bestowing these gifts the edification of the Church, and that women have received the gifts of the Spirit can be established without a doubt: then hear what these have to say.

On the day of Pentecost, when all with one accord were in one place, they heard as it were the sound of a rushing, mighty wind, and they were all filled with the Holy Ghost, and they received the gift of tongues, "and they began to speak with other tongues as the Spirit gave them [men and women] utterance." The number of them was about a hundred and twenty, and there were women among them without a doubt. It will be remembered that there is nothing said of the men that is not said of the women. "And when they were come in, they went up into an upper room, where abode both Peter, and James, and John, and Andrew, Philip and Thomas, Bartholomew, and Matthew, James, the son of Alpheus, and Simon Zelotes, and Judas the brother of James. These all continued with one accord in prayer and supplication, with the women."—Acts 1:13, 14. They were all certainly engaged in the use of the same means, and it is nothing more than reasonable to suppose that they shared alike the blessing, when it came. That the women took part in the public services of that day is evident from the language of Peter. When being reminded of the prophecy of Joel, he said, "And it shall come to pass in the last days, saith God, I will pour out of my Spirit upon all flesh, and your sons and your daughters shall prophesy [preach]." And we certify you that this gospel which they preached, was not after man; for they did not receive it of man, it came from above: they received it by the revelation of Jesus Christ. They did not confer with flesh and blood, but spake the Word with power. And just so all who have been truly regenerated and have received a gift to preach (prophesy), whether Greek or Jew, male or female, are truly commissioned as God's ministers. No others are fit for such service, though they may have complied with all the instructions of some ecclesiastical body and even by them been set apart.

If God pours out his Spirit upon the women, and says they shall prophesy (preach), who will dare say they shall not? Shall we not obey God rather than man? But if women fail to preach, what, then, becomes of Joel's prophecy? Can it ever be fulfilled? Of what authority is his prophecy? And, if this prophecy is never to be fulfilled, then we will have to drop this book from the sacred canon. But if it is to be fulfilled, then God sanctions women preaching. We understand that whatever prophesying means in men, it means in women.

It does seem strange that if women are not to preach that the apostle should give directions how godly women should dress when they did pray and prophesy in the church, and strange, indeed, that he should tell them in the very same letter that they were to keep silence in the church. He also tells the men how they are to dress, when they appear in public to pray or prophesy. Shall we not rather conclude that there is no contradiction in Paul's writings, but that some have applied to preaching what really points to the law. We must reconcile the Bible with itself, else it is no worth to us. We conclude that the men and women began the work of evangelizing the world, at Jerusalem, on the day of Pentecost, both being endued with power form on high, according to the great commission. Under the sanction of Jesus Christ and the Holy Ghost, they went everywhere preaching the Word, being accompanied with signs and wonders.

If the women did not preach, why were they persecuted and committed to prison? "As for Saul he made havoc of the Church, entering into every house, and, haling men and women, committed them to prison."—Acts 8:3. It must have been very common, then, for women to preach; so much so, that "Saul, yet breathing out threatenings and slaughter against the disciples of the Lord, went unto the high priest and desired of him letters to Damascus to the synagogues, that if he found any of this way, whether they were men or women, he might bring them bound to Jerusalem."—Acts 9:1, 2. So we went with the authority to take the women as well as the men; and Paul said, after his conversion, "And I persecuted this way unto the death, binding and delivering into prisons both men and women. As also the high priest doth bear me witness, and all the estate of the elders; from whom also I received letters unto the brethren, and went unto Damascus, to bring them which were there bound, unto Jerusalem for to be punished."—Acts 22:4, 5. We all believe that these men were persecuted, bound and imprisoned because of their zeal for Christ, and for their fidelity to his cause; and because they ceased not to preach and to teach in his name. Have we not the same reason to believe that these women were evil entreated and imprisoned for the same cause? They (as in case of the men) were captured in the synagogues and led to prison and compelled to blaspheme; and they were persecuted even unto strange cities."—Acts 26:10, 11. Yet some would have us believe that woman suffered these things because of her silence, but the Scriptures do not teach us that the silent ones suffered. Those who taught and preached in his name, whether men or women, were imprisoned and put to death, Paul himself being judge, and the high priest, elders and people being the witnesses.

> "Not she with trait'rous kiss her Master stung;
> Not she denied Him with unfaithful tongue:
> She, when apostles fled, could danger brave;
> Last at His cross, and earliest at His grave."

## "BEHOLD I HAVE SET BEFORE THEE AN OPEN DOOR."

### Rev. 3:8

——o——

Christ reveals himself to us as "the way, the truth, and the life," and as the door through which we are to enter heaven. "By me if any man enter in, he shall be saved, and shall go in and out and find pasture." All who pass this way, or come in by Christ, are equal sharers in the privileges and blessings that have been purchased by him. Because of this open door the "Star of Hope" is shining; her rays of light are flashing along the world's pathway; we, too, "have seen his star in the east and are come to worship him." This is the most beautiful star that was ever set in the heavens; the most brilliant that has ever shone; and it tells the most wonderful story ever heard. This star is composed of five points, whose rays all merge into one; they borrow their light from Him who sits upon the throne, even from Him whose birth it proclaims. Shine on, O star! Thou didst once light the plains of Bethlehem. Shine on the earth girdled with blood. Shine on the door that is open. Shine on the world redeemed to God. Shine on all the hearts of the children of men. Dark indeed must be the night, or the heart, which has not been penetrated by at least one of thy rays of light. In the person of Christ all thy beams center, and from him they will never cease to shine. God has left on record five beautiful characters, and each has an attribute of the "Sun of Righteousness." Their united rays make a star which shall shine on forever and ever.

These five illustrious and noble women are so linked together that they shed their benign light upon the page of inspiration, and all, point us to Christ "the light of the world." The brightness of their light is dazzling; we dare not look upon it as a whole; but rather upon one point or ray at a time. Oh! that our vision may be strengthened, and that we too, in the light which God giveth, may see his star clearly, and be moved with holy reverence to come and worship Him to whom these five rays point.

The first ray of light points backward to Jephthah's daughter and forward to Christ. In her case we are taught to respect the binding force of a vow; and to submit to suffering and death to preserve the sanctity of the same. (Judges 11 ch.) By the sacrifice of this noble and heroic woman, we are taught this lesson: "Offer unto God thanksgiving; and pay thy vows unto the most High." Her father, Jephthah, was a resident of Mizpeh, in the mountains of Gilead, a warrior, and a man of decided personal character. Being called upon in the extremity of his country's trials to go at the head of its armies, and to resist the Ammonites, he prepared his household for the campaign, not knowing but it might cost him his life. Being a man of prayer, he committed himself to God. He laid himself and his all upon God's altar. "Jephthah uttered all his word before the Lord in Mizpeh," and being in a great strait he promised the Lord, if he would without fail give the children of Ammon into his hand, then it should be that whatsoever came forth out of the doors of his house to meet him when he returned in peace from the battle, should be the Lord's, and it should be offered up as a burnt-offering.

He went forth to the battle, having kissed his wife and only daughter good-bye. After many hard struggles, long days and lonely nights, the shout of victory went up from their midst. God had redeemed his people. In the morning the loving husband and father hastened home with the praise of a grateful nation upon his track. When he reached the hill that overlooked his dwelling he halted; for now the full purport of his vow stood out before him. The Lord had given him the victory, and now that he was once more nearing his home he remembered his promise: "Whatsoever cometh forth of the doors of my house to meet me . . . shall surely be the Lord's, and I will offer it up for a burnt-offering." A moment more and the door opened. Jephthah looked and his eyes met those of his daughter—the one in whose existence his life was bound up. The sacred narrative says, "His daughter came out to meet him with timbrels and with dances," as if rejoicing over the redemption of Israel. It was enough, overcome with grief, Jephthah rent his clothes, and in anguish of heart cried, "Alas, my daughter! thou has brought me very low; . . . for I have opened my mouth unto the Lord and I cannot go back." His daughter then cast away her instruments of rejoicing; came forward in solemnity and answered: "My father, if thou hast opened thy mouth unto the Lord, do to me according to that which hath proceeded out of thy mouth." Here we see this grand woman offering herself freely, and dying to redeem her father's honor. With her face turned toward the heavens, she invited the fatal blow: it came; the spirit of Adah mounted up to the heavens, upon which her last gaze was fixed. The deed was done, and the name of Jephthah's daughter will forever remain famous in the annals of Scripture.

In the history of this heroic woman, who gave her life to vindicate her father's word, we have vividly brought before our minds the promised redemption through Christ. God said that the seed of the woman should bruise the serpent's head. In the fulfillment of this promise, "we see Jesus, who was made a little lower than the angels for the suffering of death." "He is the propitiation for our sins: and not for ours only, but also for the sins of the whole world." The sword which was the instrument of her death, reminds us that they came out against Christ with swords and with staves. He, too, invited the fatal blow: it came; he passed out and now appears in the presence of the Father for us. We have a faithful high priest, one that is easily "touched with the feelings of our infirmities."

Then, "like apples of gold in pictures of silver," we have set in this star the thrilling story of Ruth, the Moabitess, who forsook home and parents, land and friends, through piety to God; esteeming the reproaches of Christ greater riches than all the treasures home and friends could give. The Moabites were an idolatrous people, but she married a man named Mahlon, formerly a citizen of Bethlehem, who at that time resided in the land of Moab. He was a God-fearing man, and by his pious example and earnest efforts, influenced his wife to accept the true religion. When he came to die, he admonished her to leave the dangerous company in which she would be thrown, and to go to Bethlehem where dwelt the people of God. Soon after his death she obeyed his injunctions; she forsook home and friends, and journeyed in company with her aged mother-in-law to Bethlehem. It was the time of harvest, and she was so poor that she was compelled to go into the fields, and glean among the lowest classes for a support. Her strength was soon exhausted, for the labor was too great for her; so worn and weary, with only two little handfuls as the fruit of her day's work, she sought a place of rest. After a while Boaz (whom she expected to order her away) approached and said, "Whose damsel is this?" She raised her hands, as if to show how little were her gleanings, and that she had taken nothing from the sheaves, and placed them meekly on her breast. Thus showing a willingness to submit to anything she might be called upon to endure, she turned her eyes upward, as if appealing to God, for whom she had forsaken home, wealth, and friends. Alone in the world, she had none but God to look to for protection. This mute appeal was not lost on the kind heart of Boaz; he bade her eat and drink, and encouraged her in her work; and in a short time after this she became his wife. She has became famous in the genealogy of our Lord; for she became the mother of Obed, the father of Jesse, the father of David, the father of Solomon.

When we consider the poverty of this woman, we are reminded of Christ, who, "though he was rich, yet for your sakes he became poor, that ye through his poverty might be made rich." When we see her sheaf, we call to mind the promise, "He that goeth forth and weepeth, bearing precious seed, shall doubtless come again with rejoicing, bringing his sheaves with him.—Psa. 126:6. (See Ruth 2, 3 chs.) Ruth left her home and went to Bethlehem; Christ left heaven and came to Bethlehem. How appropriately the star hung over Bethlehem!

The third point in order, directs us to the story of queen Esther, who by going before the throne and making intercession for her people, saved them from their impending doom. (See Esther 3, 4, 5 chs). This heroine was a Jewish damsel of the tribe of Benjamin, and lived about five hundred years before the Christian era. Her parents being dead, Mordecai, her uncle, took care of her and brought her up as his own daughter. She was married in early life to king Ahasuerus. She was a very beautiful woman, and her virtues secured his love, and her wonderful genius his permanent admiration and respect. No woman has ever left behind her a better record of wisdom. As Solomon among men, so is Esther among women—the wisest of her sex. There was no problem of state so intricate that she could not help to solve it.

In time she became the king's confidante and shared with him in the greatness of his kingdom. This fact enabled her, in a season of peril, to save her nation from destruction. The enemies of the Jews being numerous and fierce against them, accused them falsely, and persuaded the king to utter an edict and to fix the day to have the race exterminated. This done, the chosen people of God were doomed to die. When queen Esther heard of this she resolved at once to make an effort to save her people at the risk of her life. There was a law to put any to death, who would essay to go in unbidden before the king when he was on his throne. But he had promised Esther that whatsoever she would ask him should be given her to the half of his kingdom. She was resolved to test his sincerity at the risk of her own life, and appealed to him to reverse the horrible edict. As she passed through the hall the sentinels handed her a copy of the law and warned her of her danger, but unmoved she bade them stand aside. Pale, yet firm, she passed through the vestibule into the great council chamber. The scene was magnificent; the king was upon the throne of gold and ivory; the splendor of the apartment, the brightness of the lights; the gorgeous equipment of his officers is rarely surpassed. Through the crowd of courtiers and the splendor of the apartment, the queen boldly passed, and in death-like silence pressed her way toward the throne, and fixed her eyes on the king, who, angry at the violation of the law, frowned sternly upon her. It was the crisis of her life, and fully realizing this fact she at once reminded him of his pledge. Rising from her humble position before the throne she saw the golden scepter bent toward her, whereupon she hastened to touch it. As the king took her by the hand and gave her a place on the throne beside him, he graciously said, "What wilt thou, queen Esther? and what is thy request? it shall be even given to thee to the half of the kingdom." Whereupon she continued her intercession for her people, and achieved a great victory in saving them.

We are reminded in the history of this woman of the fact that when justice cried for our blood, and the law had said, "The soul that sinneth it shall die," that mercy came in disguise and spread for us His bleeding hands. The Father saw it and remembered his promise, "He shall see of the travail of his soul and shall be satisfied;" and Jesus interceding said, Let man live, and the Father said, Let him live. Because He lives we shall live also. The crown by which Esther attracted the notice of the king brings to our remembrance the crown of thorns which Jesus wore while bearing the cross. The scepter points us to the fact that through his suffering on the cross pardon is to be granted, and we are to be made "kings and priests to God," and are to share in the glory of his kingdom.

The fourth point in this star we will consider under the title of Martha, who in the hour of trial possessed undeviating faith. Her heart was so fixed, and her faith so firm in God, that even death could not shake it.—John 11 ch. Her brother Lazarus was a resident of Bethany—a man of good standing among his fellow citizens, and a friend of Jesus. His house was often the resting place of Him at whose feet Mary delighted to sit. This family seemed to be very happy with the friendship of Jesus, but upon one occasion, when the Master was away, Lazarus took very sick; the sisters hastened to send him the message, "Lord, behold he whom thou lovest is sick." The Savior did not come. So Lazarus died and was buried. Four days of mourning passed, yet Martha retained her faith and trusted in him yet to come and restore the brother she had lost. In the evening of the fourth day the news came that Jesus was returning to Bethany. Martha arose and hastened to meet him and fell on her knees before him and raised her hands imploringly toward his face, and with a trembling voice, said, "Lord, if thou hadst been here my brother had not died. But I know that even now, whatsoever thou wilt ask of God, God will give it thee." Amazing faith! heroic spirit of confidence in God! Such faith was crowned with the blessings of heaven. "Jesus said unto her, Thy brother shall rise again;" upon which she replied, "I know that he shall rise again in the resurrection at the last day." "Jesus said, I am the resurrection, and the life; he that believeth in me, though he were dead, yet shall he live: and whosoever liveth and believeth in me shall never die. Believest thou this?" Well might she answer, "Yea, Lord: I believe that thou art the Christ and Son of God."

Here we are reminded by the broken column, of Christ's broken body; and by the resurrection of Lazarus, of his open tomb; and by the comforting of Martha, of the time when all the families of earth, made one in him, shall be reunited and sit down with Abraham, Isaac, and Jacob in the kingdom of heaven.

The fifth and last point directs us to Electa. "And now I beseech thee, lady, not as though I wrote a new commandment unto thee, but that which we had from the beginning, that we love one another.—II. John 1:5. We are taught to be patient and submissive under wrongs. This woman was a lady of high repute, and of a noble and wealthy family, and she lived in the days of St. John the Evangelist. She was a converted heathen. The idols of Rome were the gods she was taught to worship. Like Ruth she turned from these to the living God. She professed before the world her faith in the despised Nazarene, yet she knew well when she did so, she would be exposed to persecution and perhaps death. History tells us that fourteen years passed and then the trial came. Her house had been the home of the poor; her hands were stretched out to the needy; but the time of her martyrdom drew near and a great persecution began, and any one who professed the name of Jesus was required to recant his faith or suffer the penalty of the law. Electa, as were others, was visited by the soldiers who proposed the test of casting a cross on the ground, and of requiring her to put her foot on it. This she refused to do, and she and her family were cast into a dungeon for one year, after which the Roman judge came and offered her another opportunity to recant her faith, promising if she would, she should be protected. Again she refused, and this brought the drama to a speedy close. The whole family were scourged to the very verge of death. Then they were drawn on a cart by oxen to the nearest hill and crucified. She saw her husband perish; she saw each of her children die on the cruel tree; she was then nailed there herself, and thus sealed her faith with her blood.

Her cross reminds us of Him who went that way before her. The cup from which she gave the thirsty drink reminds us of the bitter cup which he drank for us, and of the cup he gave us in memory of his death. The clasped hands remind us of his love. "Love one another as I have loved you."

In looking at this star we are pointed to Christ by every ray and by every symbol. On the body of this star we have first the open Bible, which is the testament of the great Testator, and by this we are pointed to him. In the light of the second ray, represented by the bunch of lilies, we are pointed to Christ as the "Lily of the Valley," who in this light is "the fairest among ten thousand and altogether lovely." In the third ray, represented by the sun shining in his strength, we are referred to him as the "Sun of Righteousness." "For the Lord God is a sun and shield." In the fourth symbol or ray, we have the lamb and the cross. Nothing could be more appropriate, since by these we are pointed to Christ, "the Lamb of God which taketh away the sins of the world." "He is brought as a lamb to the slaughter, and as a sheep before her shearers is dumb, so he opened not his mouth." "He was cut out of the land of the living; for the transgression of my people was he stricken." We shall overcome by the blood of the Lamb. In the last emblem on the body of this star, we see the lion which points us to him that spake, even to the Man of sorrows, the Lion of the tribe of Judah, which took the book and opened the seven seals, and in that open book we read he uttered while on the cross seven sentences.

On each of these five points we have an emblem which is still pointing Christward: first, the sword and the veil. By these we are reminded that they came out against Christ with swords and staves, and took him, and nailed him to the cross; and that amid rending rocks and opening tombs, the veil of the temple was rent in twain, while the sun veiled himself in darkness, and they pierced his side with a sword. We have also the sheaf, pointing us to the promise, "He shall see the travail of his soul, and shall be satisfied; by his knowledge shall my righteous servant justify many." The fields are truly white unto the harvest. The crown and scepter point us to him that is crowned King of kings and Lord of lords—even to him whose sceptre pardon gives—who shall reign until all enemies are put under his feet. The broken column reminds us of his horrible death. In the midst of life he was cut off in death, and "numbered with the transgressors." Lastly, we have the cup and joined hands pointing us to the bitter cup he drank, and to his love for us when he said, "Behold, I stand at the door and knock; if any man hear my voice and open the door, I will come in to him, and will sup with him and he with me."

To give this star a finishing touch, we paint in five colors—blue, yellow, white, green, and red. The blue is an emblem of truth; the yellow, of jealousy—"God is a jealous God"; white is an emblem of purity—God is so pure that even "the heavens are not clean in his sight;" green, an emblem of loneliness, means forsaken—"My God, my God! why hast thou forsaken me!" the red is an emblem of love.

Again, by the blue we are pointed to Him that "sitteth upon the circles of the earth;" who plants his foot upon the deep blue sea and rideth upon the storm, and stills us to rest as a mother stills her child upon her breast. By the yellow we are reminded of his command, "Go work in my vineyard;" for "the harvest truly is great, but the laborers are few," and whosoever will, may gather fruit unto life eternal. The yellow says, "Put ye in the sickle, for the harvest is ripe." White—Oh what a beautiful type of Him in whose mouth no guile was found. He rides upon a white horse clothed in brightness. He shineth as the sun in his strength, for in him there is "no darkness at all." In the green we have the hope of the resurrection. For by this we are reminded that he died and rose again; and that now he ever lives, and because he lives we shall live also. For the promise is, "Whosoever liveth and believeth on me shall never die." "I shall be satisfied when I awake with his likeness." The last ray in this star (the red) points us to his love, and "herein is love, not that we loved God, but that he loved us and gave himself for us." As we look upon the red, represented by the rose, we are pointed to Christ as "the Rose of Sharon." When he shed his blood his love to show, he girdled the earth with the crimson tide. We go back to the blue to see the heavens receive him out of sight, and the blood cries out, Look up to God! As the rays of light fall on the open book, we read and admire the characters of those heroic women, who, by their noble deeds, faith, zeal and courage, have rendered their names immortal. We would recommend the lives of these noble women to the world as being worthy of imitation. So let each one that reads these lines try to cultivate the virtues and graces of the tried and chosen servants of God. Let each one practice them in his life, and point to Christ as these did, and are yet pointing to him. The deeds of these women will never die; their names will ever be held in gracious remembrance; as we try to rob Death of his prey, as to try to rob these of immortality. "Thy people shall be my people, and thy God my God."

*F.A.T.A.L.*

## "AND THEY CAME, BOTH MEN AND WOMEN, AS MANY AS WERE WILLING-HEARTED," Etc.

### Ex. 35:22

——o——

After the captivity of the children of Israel, they returned to Jerusalem, and under the direction of Nehemiah, the walls of the city were rebuilt, in the twentieth year of the reign of Artaxerxes. "So I came to Jerusalem, and was there three days. And I arose in the night, I and some few men with me; neither told I any man what my God had put in my heart to do at Jerusalem"—Neh. 2:11, 12. The prophet "went up in the night . . . and viewed the wall," "and the rulers knew not whither he went." He gathered all the people together. "And all the congregation of them that were come again out of the captivity made booths, and sat under the booths. . . . And there was very great gladness." "And all the people gathered themselves together as one man into the street that was before the water gate, and they spake unto Ezra the scribe to bring the book of the law of Moses, which the Lord had commanded to Israel. And Ezra the priest brought the law before the congregation both of men and women, and all that could hear with understanding, upon the first day of the seventh month. And he read therein before the street that was before the water gate, from the morning until mid-day, before the men and the women and those that could understand; and the ears of all the people were attentive unto the book of the law. And Ezra the scribe stood upon a pulpit of wood which they had made for the purpose. . . . And Ezra opened the book in the sight of all the people (for he was above all the people); and when he opened it all the people stood up: and Ezra blessed the Lord, the great God. And all the people answered, Amen, Amen, with lifting up their hands: and they bowed their heads, and worshipped the Lord with their faces to the ground."—Neh. 8:1-6. And all the people clave together. "And the rest of the people, the priests, the Levites, the porters, the singers, the Nethinim, and all they that had separated themselves from the people of the lands unto the law of God, their wives, their sons, and their daughters, every one having knowledge, and having understanding; they clave to their brethren, their nobles, and entered into a curse, and into an oath [that is a covenant], to walk in God's law, which was given by Moses the servant of God, and to observe and do all the commandments of the Lord, our Lord, and his judgments and his statutes."—Neh. 10:28, 29.

Having thus covenanted together, men and women, to do his work and to keep his statutes, they began the work of rebuilding the walls of Jerusalem, and both shared in this great undertaking. In the third chapter of Nehemiah, we have the names and the order of them that builded the wall. The work of each one was necessary to the completion of the whole. Though their persecution was great, they continued the work. "When Sanballat heard that we builded the wall, he was wroth, and took great indignation, and mocked the Jews."—Neh. 4:1. "But it came to pass, that when Sanballat, and Tobiah, and the Arabians, and the Ammonites, and the Ashdodites, heard that the walls of Jerusalem were made up, and that the breaches began to be stopped, then they were very wroth, and conspired all of them together, to come and to fight against Jerusalem, and to hinder it."—Neh. 4:7, 8. But these men and women worked right on side by side: for the prophet "rose up, and said unto the nobles, and to the rulers, and to the rest of the people, Be not ye afraid of them: remember the Lord which is great and terrible, and fight for your brethren, your sons, and your daughters, your wives, and your houses."—Neh. 4:14. "Every one with one of his hands wrought in the work, and with the other hand held a weapon. For the builders, every one, had a sword girded by his side, and so builded."—Neh. 4:17, 18. They were ready at any time for the approach of the enemy, and at the sound of the trumpet, they were to meet the enemy in combat. So they were instructed, men and women: "In what place therefore ye hear the sound of the trumpet, resort ye thither with us: our God shall fight for us"—that is for the builders. We read, Neh. 3:12, "And next unto him repaired Shallum, the son of Halohesh, the ruler of the half part of Jerusalem, he and his daughters." If God fought for the women in building the walls of Jerusalem, will he not fight for them as they fulfill the prophecy?—"They shall build the old wastes, they shall raise up the former desolations, and they shall repair the waste cities, the desolations of many generations."—Isa. 61:4.

Woman's work in the building of the temple was recognized by man and blessed of Heaven. Shall men refuse now to recognize her as a builder, as a warrior, as a helper? Had those women failed to do their part of the work, the walls would not have been completed. The men might have done their part of the work, and have done it well; yet that would not have sufficed. The work of the women was necessary to the completion or perfection of the whole. Their work did not take from the work of the men, but rather added to it; and thus the breaches were closed. "They offered great sacrifices, and rejoiced: for God had made them rejoice with great joy: the wives also and the children rejoiced: so that the joy of Jerusalem was heard afar off."—Neh. 12:43. They pledged themselves to walk in all the commandments of the Lord their God.

Just so the men of to-day may nobly perform their part of the work in spreading the Gospel, but if the women fail to do their part, there will be a breach in the wall. Now, shall woman with her heaven-soaring aspirations, fail to consecrate her time and talents to God? "Yet now our flesh is as the flesh of our brethren, our children as their children: and, lo, we bring into bondage our sons and our daughters to be servants, and some of our daughters are brought into bondage already."—Neh. 5:5. Who, then, will help us to deliver? The storm may rage, and the tempest may howl, but when we cry aloud for help, the Master standeth near, and whispers in our souls, "It is I; be not afraid." We know he holds us by the hand, and we can trust him where'er he leads. Though the clouds be dark, and the waves beat high, he still sustains us, and far beyond the darkness, in the land of unclouded day, we shall know why in his wisdom he hath led us so.

It is said that when the house of the Lord was in building, "It was built of stone made ready before it was brought thither, so that there was neither hammer, nor ax, nor any tool of iron heard in the house, while it was in building."—I. Kings 6:7. This teaches us a spiritual lesson. All regenerated persons belong to the house of God, "and are built upon the foundation of the apostles and prophets, Jesus Christ himself being the chief cornerstone; in whom all the building fitly framed together, groweth into an holy temple in the Lord; in whom ye also are builded together for an habitation of God through the Spirit."—Eph. 2:20-22.

So there is a temple being erected, not made with hands; Christ is the foundation upon which that house is being built. He is a sure foundation—"a living stone, disallowed indeed of men, but chosen of God, and precious. Ye, also, as lively stones are built up a spiritual house, an holy priesthood, to offer up spiritual sacrifices, acceptable to God by Jesus Christ."—I. Peter 2:4, 5. If women have a place in this "spiritual house," then it follows that they are to offer up spiritual sacrifices. The sacrifice that God requires is not a dead, but a living sacrifice; that is a moving, active sacrifice, such as we may give by consecrating our lives to his service. Paul, in writing to the church at Rome, said, "I beseech you, therefore, brethren, by the mercies of God, that ye present your bodies a living sacrifice, holy, acceptable unto God, which is your reasonable service."—Rom. 12:1.

Women, coming as lively stones to Christ, the living stone, have their places side by side with the men in the spiritual house, and are as much required as they to consecrate their lives to God—not as a dead, inactive, but as a living sacrifice. They have as much right to aid in getting up the material and in building this house, as any man.

The stones in the temple were made ready before they were brought thither, and when the building was erected, the sound of the workman's hammer was not heard. So in the building of the temple of God, this spiritual house, we are not to use carnal weapons, but "The sword of the Spirit, which is the word of God." This is to be used by faith, with much prayer. "Praying always with all prayer and supplication in the Spirit, and watching thereunto with all persever-ance and supplication, for all saints." "For they watch for your souls, as they that must give account, that they may do it with joy, and not with grief." This lesson Christ taught us when "they came out against him with swords and staves" from the chief priests and elders of the people. When his disciples saw that the multitude would take him, they came to his rescue with carnal weapons. "Then Simon Peter having a sword drew it, and smote the high priest's servant, and cut off his right ear. Then said Jesus unto Peter, Put up thy sword into the sheath." "All they that take the sword shall perish with the sword."

This gentle rebuke is to us a warning. How dare we go without the anointing of the Spirit? Carnal weapons will not suffice; we must have the power of God. There are many mighty and powerful swords, but none so powerful as that which God giveth—even the sword of truth. Some of these swords glitter in the form of rhetoric, intellect, education, etc. Some ministers, in the use of their swords can rise and touch the very skies; others can dive into the depths and pierce nature's veil; but how much mightier the sword of God's. It can pierce the heart. "The Word of God is quick and powerful, and sharper than any two-edged sword, piercing to the dividing asunder of soul and spirit, and of the joints and marrow, and is a discerner of the thoughts and intents of the heart."—Heb. 4:12. Truly, "He that is joined unto the Lord is one spirit." "The God of heaven will prosper us."

## CHRISTIAN AND PAGAN WOMANHOOD.

——o——

A religion that does not give woman the liberty, privileges, and blessings, that it does man, will not stand the test; it falls far short of being the religion of the Bible. We learn from the Bible, that there are gods, many, and of course as many religions. James says, "If any man among you seem to be religious, and bridleth not his tongue, but deceiveth his own heart, this man's religion is vain." He also gives us the definition of the true religion, saying, it is "To visit the fatherless and widows in their afflictions, and to keep himself unspotted from the world." This is the only religion in which men and women are equal sharers. All others put woman below the man, and make her a slave to a greater or less extent. In heathen lands, where our Bible has not yet found its way, and where our gospel has not been heard, women are drudges. Even those in royal robes live in fear and dread of their lords and masters.

Turn, now, the dark pages of history, and we find among Babylonians, Lydians, Syrians, Persians, and many other barbarous nations, that women were sold for wives, and even for slaves. They were regarded as being but a little above the brute creation. All peoples and nations are what their religions make them. Their religions were wrong, and, consequently, the wrongs the poor women suffered were great. In Greece, woman's position was not quite so degrading; yet she was considered as fit only for menial drudgery. There is nothing sadder than the condition of woman in the decline of the Roman empire. She was so degraded that life itself became a burden. In some nations the wife is the slave of her husband, while he lives, and at his death she becomes the property of his father. In other countries she is put to death on the grave of her husband, that she may continue to serve him in another world. We are shocked when we read of such inhumanity of man toward woman, and we stand in horror of such treatment. We cease to wonder at this when we remember that this is a part of their religion.

It cannot be denied that this is the general history of women without the light of our gospel, and without the influence of our religion. Then, wherein consists the woman's, or the nation's greatness or liberty? The secret, or answer, is found in the open Bible.

It is a fact that a religion that degrades and dishonors woman does not elevate the man. On the other hand, a religion that elevates the man, will give equal honor to the woman. It is only when woman is held in high esteem, that man becomes noble and rises to true greatness. This lesson Christ taught when he came to earth, and walked with men, and ministered unto them. Herein lies true greatness. Strength is not greatness, but weakness when given, or consecrated, to God, is greatness.

In heathen nations, woman's love or preference is not considered in regard to marriage, and wives are taught to obey their husbands as lords, or even as slaves obey their masters. But our religion teaches the wives to obey their husbands through true love and affection; and the husbands to give honor to their wives as unto the weaker vessel, and to love them as Christ loved the Church, and gave himself for it. What a contrast! Heathenism teaches that a wife must be a slave; Christianity, that she is a helpmeet—an equal sharer in all the blessings of the gospel. It is true, that it took many years, and even centuries, to rid the popular mind of its time-hardened superstitious notions regarding the inferiority of woman. But a few years ago it was thought that woman was incapacitated for teaching school. However, as Christianity advances, which it is doing continually, woman becomes more and more elevated, and is found teaching in our best schools. Indeed, every true man reverences the very name of woman, and with our religion, says, liberate the woman: while heathenism, with its chains, says, she shall bear our burdens. She has her infant strapped across her back, while her lordly escort goes untrammeled.

Christianity is always ready to help the woman; it meets her at the gate; it escorts her to her room; it gives her the best chair; and when she walks, it carries her parasol. Whence comes this refinement? Is it the offspring of heathenism? Nay; 'tis the child of Christianity. To deny this, is infidelity. Though woman be weaker physically and mentally (if you choose to say it) than a man, it is admitted that in some points she is the stronger. As a rule, she is stronger to resist temptation; she is more patient and resolute. While there are many grand and noble Christian men, yet it is true, that women, with their confiding and sympathetic natures, are more easily brought to Christ; and are thereby more readily and directly benefitted by hearing the gospel. The number of Christian women far exceeds that of men.

And it is certainly true that woman's influence, whether for good or evil, is great. What the world needs most is woman's influence given to God. When the women are christianized, the world will be converted to the service of the living God. Observation gives some idea of a woman's influence. One vile, brutal woman in a village or community, will do more to corrupt morals, and bring shame and disgrace to womanhood, and the community, than a dozen men; for her ways are the ways of hell: yea, "her house is the way to hell, going down to the chambers of death." "Let not thine heart decline to her ways, go not astray in her paths. For she hath cast down many wounded: yea, many strong men have been slain by her."

Take the influence of the Christian women out of the world today; stop her in all her efforts to do good and to bring the world to Christ; forbid her to teach the way of salvation; put her to silence in the churches; and you have a Samson shorn of his locks: yea, the Church is robbed of her strength. Our house will be divided, and a few more gusts of wind, another wave, and our destruction will be sure. Woe to the world when the Church binds her women; when Christianity gives her womanhood to infidelity and heathenism; when she takes from them the privileges nothing else can give! Midnight darkness, with the shades of hell, will surround the world, and the chains that no man can break asunder will bind us. Men and morals will sink to rise no more; the floods of infamy and shame will cover us. We have need to learn that, "We, then, that are strong ought to bear the infirmities of the weak," and that men and women should work together for the glory of God and the salvation of souls. If the cause is a worthy one, we ought to use all the help we can get, and not reject the assistance of any.

That we may be able to appreciate the help of woman, and to comprehend the greatness of her influence, the reader is referred to Mrs. Dr. Finney, of the United States, who visited Edinburgh, Scotland, in 1859. At that time there was no such thing in all Scotland as a woman's prayer-meeting—indeed, a woman that would attempt to pray, even among her own sex, was thought to be very much out of place. In the Bristow Street Hall, of Brighton Street Congregation, of the Evangelical Union Church, with the co-operation of Mrs. Dr. Kirk (wife of the pastor, Rev. John Kirk), Mrs. Finney organized the first woman's prayer-meeting ever organized in Scotland. The movement was then condemned by the masses. Men and women lifted up their hands in "holy horror;" but the meeting went on, gradually increasing in interest. One by one, ladies of other denominations came in; some came to wonder and criticise, but remained to pray, and finally went away to praise. The influence of that meeting widened and deepened; prejudice gave way, and many other prayer-meetings were organized in the city; thence this movement spread to other towns, and over the whole of Scotland. To-day they have a band of workers not often excelled.

The established Church of Scotland, which is Presbyterian, has gone so far as to appoint deaconesses; and in every denomination in Scotland, the women do a large part of the church work, and especially in collecting funds for missionary purposes. Not only so, but they speak in public in the churches. It is said that three of the best speakers ever heard in Edinburgh were women. Right will finally triumph. Though this woman's prayer-meeting met with great opposition, these faithful women have brought all Scotland to their way of thinking. Who would have thought of the third great Scottish Reformation's having an American origin—and only a woman for its author! Who could have believed that a woman could set so many wheels to turning in this so grand a movement?

The battle is waxing hotter, the tempest is howling louder, and Satan must be cast out. With a few more Mrs. Finneys, and Elizabeth Frys, the contest will be over, and the victory will be ours. They are coming; the tide is already upon us; and he that cannot read the signs of the times must be asleep to the surroundings. Who knows what a sensation the next movement may create? The women are fast coming to the front, and are engaging in active public work. Already a large majority of Sunday-school teachers and officers are women. But she has not yet attained to all that is her rightful possession and privilege. It is only a question of time when she will stand at the top. Though many obstacles are thrown in her way, it only remains for time to show that these will disappear as mists before the rising sun. God will wipe them away as so many cobwebs. It is certain that no amount of prejudice, and narrow-heartedness and opposition, can very long keep back the in-coming flood. Women will not always be held back by these things. Many good and noble ones have been cried down, but when once the door is open others will enter.

The world is moving; time is flying, and souls are dying: and the church must move, or the blood of many will be on her skirts. There are already many women, of no mean ability, of various denominations, who speak clearly and distinctly. They have opened their mouths, and they will not go back; and the church that cuts them off inflicts on herself a wound that time will not, yea cannot, heal. No church, awake to its interests, and alive to the cause of Christ, can afford to do such a thing. This forward religious movement of the women has started a wave that will touch all denominations. It will sweep over every plain; it shall increase for good; dashing down the hillside of time, it shall strike the shore of eternity, to meet many thousands, who will bless God for the good and noble women that shared in this great work. Woman's mission is to reach the noble and the sublime, and unless she succeeds in making the world better and happier, by her work and by her life, she fails to attain unto the high standard assigned her. She may teach holy truths, and point souls to the Rock of Ages, everywhere—in the Sabbath-school, in the church, in the crowded tenement houses of great cities, and in the harems of India. If she fails in this work, the luster of her womanhood's glory is dimmed thereby.

Let her be careful in using her best gifts for Christ (who was ever the friend of woman), and his service. While heathen voices, from all parts of the Orient, are heard crying for the bread of life, may not the hearts of many be thrilled, who will arise and obey the Lord's command: "Go work in my vineyard," and, "as ye go, preach?" May not our women, like Mary, choose to set at the feet of the Master, and be as much honored as she that is "cumbered about much serving?" Women of culture and refinement are needed to go as gospel messengers to the nations that "sit in darkness."

There are many reasons why women should go to the foreign field of labor, as well as remain at home, but I will give only two. First; Because of the acknowledged, exalted position conferred by Christ and the gospel upon womanhood. Second; Because of her influence, and because of certain social customs, which abound in many heathen countries, which customs prevent women from being reached except by their own sex. So far her labors in this respect have been wonderfully blessed. In the last few years, women in their work, have made a record that ought to inspire them with greater courage in coming time. To work among the heathen, many women have left home, and friends, and native land, perhaps never to see those dear unto them, until their mission on earth is accomplished and they receive their star-decked crowns in the New Jerusalem. But, God's watchful eye is over them; his boundless love enfolds them; his everlasting arm is underneath them: and they are borne up amid all the conflicts of life. Any effort to hold woman back in this great work, is but a step downward, and all opposition may be attributed, either to a misunderstanding of the Scriptures, or to downright prejudice—either of which is hurtful to the cause, and tends toward heathenism.

Again, that we may have a better idea of the vastness of woman's influence, we refer to Jezebel, the wife of king Ahab. (See I. Kings 21:1-17.) That wicked woman had Naboth "stoned with stones that he died," and after his death she influenced Ahab to take (steal) his vineyard. Ahab was a bad man, but Jezebel was a worse woman. When his plans failed, she manufactured lies and devised plots for the death of Naboth; and she succeeded. That a bad woman is worse than a bad man, and that her influence is greater than his, is demonstrated in this instance. She was determined to have Naboth's vineyard, and nothing stood in her way. She laid a scheme for disposing of him, under the garb of religion. She had a fast proclaimed: Naboth was set on high, as a man of recognized position and piety; then wicked and worthless men accused him of blasphemy, which meant death under the law of Moses. The awful deed was done, and in the name of religion, this wicked woman had an innocent man murdered. By reason of her influence, Ahab took possession of the coveted vineyard.

In order to fathom the depth of woman's degradation and misery in heathen darkness, we will refer the reader to history. Women in the primitive era of the Romans were held in perpetual minority. When they passed from the hands of their fathers to their husbands, they simply became the property of another, and were placed under perpetual guardianship. (See Ortolan's History of Roman Law.) "All women, on account of the infirmity of their judgments, shall be under the power, or control, of tutors." —Cicero. The Voconian Law prohibited a man from making a woman, even an only daughter, his heir.—Augustine. Indeed, a woman was not allowed to own any property at all. She had no right, at any age, to control her own time, or regulate her own conduct. All her earnings belonged to her father, or, if he were dead, to a brother, or some representative of the stronger sex. And if any one, at her marriage, bestowed upon her a gift, it became at once the property of her husband. She had no control over anything, not even over her own children. The father could give away her daughters without her consent. Even in widowhood, a woman could not become the guardian of her own children. She could not inherit property by will. Such laws, to civilized people, seem worse than barbarous. All that has been said of Rome applies to Greece. Perpetual minority was the highest boon given by them to woman. Women did all the drudgery: they could make no bargain that was legal; not even purchase their own apparel with their own earnings. In fact, a woman was not allowed to have any religion except that prescribed by her master.

Concerning woman's position in ancient India, the Shasters, or sacred books of the Hindoos, are the best authority. From them we quote: "By a girl, or a young woman, or a woman advanced in years, nothing must be done, even in her own dwelling, according to her wishes, or mere pleasure. When in the presence of her husband, she must abandon everything else, and be ready to receive his commands." She is even kept in subjection by means of a rope, or a small cane; and it is believed, so far as she honors her husband, so far will she be exalted in heaven. In vain we try to fathom the depths of such degradation; for Christian womanhood cannot comprehend it. Think, will you, of a woman with heaven-soaring aspirations, being thus compelled to bow to her lord and master (man). It is worse than an outrage, and but for an open Bible, and its blessed influence, the daughters of America would be bound with heavy chains.

Among many of the Greeks, and other nations, polygamy was practiced, and had the sanction of the law. A stream can not rise higher than the fountain from which it proceeds, therefore, when the basis of such degradation is considered (woman's inferiority), we do not wonder that the course is downward. Many testimonies like the above could be given, but these are fair samples, and will serve our purpose. But why should woman be thus cribbed and fettered? Heathenism answers, "Because of her inferiority."

What the Church most needs, is to arise, with sword in hand, to cut off the head of this great monster. Will she do it? If she fails, she fails in her high mission; for every effort that is being made to break these chains, and to liberate woman, is in accord with the great commission: "Go ye, therefore, and teach all nations." Shall we, then, go over and possess the land? To this the Church replies, we will; and she sends out her missionaries, and thereby says, our women are free. Truly they are free; for "If the Son, therefore, shall make you free, ye shall be free indeed." "Where the Spirit of the Lord is, there is liberty."—II. Cor. 3:17. We are free to serve God, as moved by the

Spirit, without respect of persons—both men and women. There is nothing said of woman's being bound, and man's being liberated. Yet, if she is to be kept in subjection, and not allowed to speak, then where is her liberty?

Beware, O man, lest thou become a usurper in binding what God hath loosed, and thou be found fighting against God! Remember, just as thou art free, so woman is free; and as thou standest, she stands. "Take heed, lest by any means, this liberty of yours become a stumbling-block to them that are weak."—I. Cor. 8:9. "As free, and not using your liberty for a cloak of maliciousness, but as the servants of God." "Stand fast, therefore, in the liberty wherewith Christ hath made us free." "Brethren, ye have been called unto liberty; only use not liberty for an occasion to the flesh, but by love serve one another."—Gal. 5:13. These admonitions, many would do well to read, and then to see to it that they do not put a stumbling-block in somebody else's way, by putting ecclesiastical restrictions on women's mouths.

"The Lord will provide," is as true now as when first uttered. There is a power behind the throne, and help will yet come. The foe shall be cast out; Haman shall be hanged. This modern Haman, like Haman of old, offers to pay for cutting off our women; saying, I will give them to you in everlasting bondage; her chains shall be upon your daughters, and her fetters upon your grand-daughters. He places his feet on the American shores, and holds out his hand to the Church, and offers himself in holy wedlock. Strange that our Church will adopt the sentiment of the wicked Persian monarch, and say, Do with them as it seemeth good. Who can believe that she will do thus? Yet those who would hinder women in the spread of the gospel, are promising this modern Haman their assistance. Who knows but this gallows is the very one upon which they shall be hanged? The world has already felt the tread of an Esther, and through her instrumentality the world's womanhood shall be redeemed. The edict shall be changed; the chains shall be broken; and woman shall be at liberty to work for God, in "The land of the free, and the home of the brave." Our extremities have ever been God's opportunities. The ravens fed Elijah when he was in need. It does not matter whether they were birds or men, they came at the right time. Paul says, "All things are yours," and the Lord said, "The barrel of meal shall not waste, neither shall the cruse of oil fail." "And the king said unto Esther, What is thy petition? and it shall be granted thee: and what is thy request? even to the half of the kingdom it shall be performed."—Esth. 5:6. Jesus said, "Ask, and it shall be given you." "For ever, O Lord, thy word is settled in heaven," "Rejoice, O heaven, and sing, O earth;" for God hath said, "O woman, great is thy faith; be it unto thee even as thou wilt." Esther with God has prevailed, and my people, men and women, are free.

The outlook is truly encouraging. The women of America have accomplished a work in the last decade of which they may well be proud. The record they have made is cheering, and soul-inspiring. Many doors of usefulness have been opened to them, and women everywhere are preparing themselves to explore fields where their tread has never yet been felt. These are stubborn and unyielding facts, and ere long we will have passed the milestone that says, put a padlock on woman's lips. Miriam and Moses shall again stand side by side in this great conflict. "For we wrestle not against flesh and blood, but against principalities, against powers, . . . against spiritual wickedness in high places." Already a number of noble women are in the field, and others are on the threshhold.

Within the last half century, the cause of female education has made wonderful progress. Female colleges abound in all parts of the country, and their number is rapidly increasing. Woman may now make choice of her employment, and educate herself for the same. In the near future the voice of the croaker will be hushed. Two-thirds of our public schools are now taught by women, and they have proved themselves efficient teachers. The stupid prejudices which have been holding women back, are fast giving way. From the Nazareths of America women are coming whose influence will be felt from pole to pole.

Mrs. Annie C. Peyton, of Mississippi, has founded an industrial institute and college at Columbus, Miss. In spite of great and seemingly insurmountable obstacles, Elizabeth Blackwell has won great renown in her chosen calling, and she has lived to see many medical schools established even in America. Such institutions may be found in Chicago, Philadelphia, New York, Boston, and Cleveland. These institutions have sent out hundreds of graduates, who are an honor to their profession, and for skill they are not a whit behind the men of the same calling. From the work of such women as Frances E. Willard, Dora T. Lanthrop, Sallie F. Chapin, Dora Read Goodall, Sarah Crosby, Mary Bosanquet, Mrs. Frame, and many others, we have invincible proof that they have received the anointing of the

Holy Spirit. They were no doubt called of God, and heaven-ordained messengers; for "by their fruits ye shall know them."

In January, 1861, the first Woman's Missionary Society was organized, and it was non-sectarian. In 1868 the Woman's Board of Missions, auxiliary to the American Board, came into existence. In 1869 the Woman's Missionary Society of the Methodist Episcopal Church was organized. The Presbyterian Church organized a similar society in 1870; the Baptist in 1871; the Protestant Episcopal Church in 1872; the Methodist Episcopal Church, South, in 1878; and the Cumberland Presbyterian Church in 1880. Since then other churches have followed these examples, and there are now twenty-two such organizations among the various denominations. "Behold, how great a matter a little fire kindleth." We leave the reader to consider the work of these societies.

Again, in 1887, the Church of Scotland, through its General Assembly, created the office of deaconess, and a school for the training of women for that office has been established in Edinburgh. The movement in America is certainly pointing in that direction, and in many of our churches women are doing the work of deacons. If she does the work that pertains to an office, is there any reason why she should not hold that office? It is certain that many of them can do the work that pertains to the office more successfully than many of our men. These are stern facts, and why women should not be clothed officially for this work, is a thought difficult of conception. To be consistent, the Church should either take this work out of woman's hands, or clothe her with this authority. Which will she do? To take this work out of her hands, she slays her best collecting agents, and her finances, or income, will be cut short. To clothe her with official authority, is but to open the way for her ordination to the gospel ministry.

Woman's prospect for future usefulness is brightening: new fields are inviting her: and when she has once entered the work, no earthly power can turn the tide. Who can put the machinery into operation that will stop the temperance work, or the work of our Woman's Board, or of the various societies? In our own Church, in various congregations, and in different presbyteries, women are acting as deacons and clerks of sessions. All this is but admitting that she is capable of doing the work that pertains to these offices. And if she does the work successfully, why not let her hold the office? Can any reason be given, except that of the man who plowed with a crooked stick?—" 'cause dad plowed that way!" This is an age of improvement, and the days of wooden plows have been left behind; and the man that does this or that " 'cause dad did it," is unwilling to make any progress. He is but a modern Rip Van Winkle.

This is only priming the picture. If the channels of woman's usefulness are ever filled up, many great and deep fountains of charity and blessedness will forever cease to flow. The current of salvation will be turned backward, and our sisters of the Orient will be doomed to perpetual bondage. But Thou, O God, canst work, and none can hinder. Thou canst break the chains, and set these poor women free. Earth shall yet keep her jubilee. God has opened to woman a door of usefulness—and no man can shut it. How many say, "Here am I, send me!"

## "THE TRUTH SHALL MAKE YOU FREE."
——o——

"The Lord gave the Word: great was the company of those that published it. Kings of armies did flee apace: and she that tarried at home divided the spoil."—Psa. 68:11,12. Here it is said, that the Lord gave the Word, and great was the number that published, or preached, that Word. By reference to the first chapter of the gospel as recorded by John, we have the definition of the word, which John says was in the beginning with God, and by whom all things were made. "The Word was made flesh, and dwelt among us, and we beheld his glory, the glory as of the only begotten of the Father, full of grace and truth."—John 1:14. This is the Word given by God, and that which we were admonished by Paul to preach. It is also stated that, "She that tarried at home divided the spoil." It seems that the prophet Jeremiah had an eye single to this fact when he said: "Consider ye, and call for the mourning women, that they may come; and send for the cunning women that they may come; and let them make haste, and take up a wailing for us, that our eyes may run down with tears, and our eyelids gush out with waters. For a voice of wailing is heard out of Zion. How are we spoiled! we are greatly confounded."—Jer. 9:17-19. You see the Word is to be published, and the spoil divided, and the prophet has called for the woman. Zion is spoken of as the Church, and it seems here that her banners were trailing in the dust, that she was groping her way in darkness. We feel sure that these women went into the work remembering the promise that when Zion travailed, that sons and daughters should be born unto her. Let us here ask these, "Watchman, what of the night?" Can we not truthfully say, the day breaketh and the morning dawneth, and thereby join Isaiah the prophet, and say, "Rise up, ye women that are at ease; hear my voice, ye careless daughters; give ear unto my speech. Many days and years shall ye be troubled, ye careless women: for the vintage shall fail, and the gathering shall not come. Tremble ye women that are at ease; be troubled, ye careless ones. Upon the land of my people shall come up thorns and briers; yea, upon all the houses of joy in the joyous city."—Isa. 32:9-13. If there was ever a time when we ought to be up and doing, surely it is now: wickedness, vice and folly, immorality and sins of the deepest dye, rise up to choke the Word. Would we not do well in this age of improvement, to get out of the old ruts, and to shake off the chains of prejudice? "Stand ye in the ways, and see and ask for the old paths, where is the good way, and walk therein." Now, as these men were moved by the Holy Ghost, they spake, being a mouth-piece for God, and they prophesied of things to come. They, while under the influence of the Holy Ghost, spoke and wrote not of nor for themselves, but of, and for God. So let us hear what these say. Now, if woman's true place is at home, why did this prophet call for them? Why burden them unnecessarily? Did he make a mistake when he called for the woman? The truth is, woman has ever been regarded by holy men, and by God, as an important factor in the beginning and completion of the world's redemption. To her the promise was made, and by her the world was presented with a Savior which was indeed the Christ, who, by his triumphant death and resurrection, conquered death, hell and the grave. And because he ever liveth, we expect to conquer through the seed of the woman; and he hath called us to glory and to virtue.

Solomon said, "Open thy mouth for the dumb in the cause of all such as are appointed to destruction."—Prov. 31:8. Now, if the above read thus, Open thy mouth in the interest of the dumb, etc., the meaning would not be changed, and we think it would be a better rendering. Again, same chapter, verse 9, "Open thy mouth, judge righteously, and plead the cause of the poor and needy." Here the women are directed, through the organ of speech, to address the poor and needy, or, as David has it, present them with the Word which the Lord gave; and Paul calls it preaching the Word. The price of such a woman is "far above rubies." "Strength and honor are her clothing; and she shall rejoice in time to come. She openeth her mouth with wisdom, and in her tongue is the law of kindness" (verses 10, 25, 26). That women have been called upon to open their mouths and speak in the interest of the poor and needy, is in keeping with the New Testament. Christ would always have the poor remembered, and when he made a great supper, he directed his servants (whether men or women) to "go out into the streets and lanes of the city, and bring in hither the poor and the maimed, and the halt and the blind." Surely a more needy people could not be found, yet this is the class among whom these women were directed to labor. The Lord has promised them, that "No weapon that is formed against them shall prosper, and every tongue that shall rise against them in judgment they should condemn."—Isa. 54:17.

"Yet hear the word of the Lord, O ye women, and let your ear receive the word of his mouth, and teach your daughters wailing, and every one her neighbor lamentation."—Jer. 9:20. Here women are commanded to receive the Word of the Lord—the same Word that Paul said preach. They are to teach or preach it, first to their children, and then to their neighbors. Here we may ask, and "Who is my neighbor?" The reader will remember the unfortunate man who fell among the thieves, and the action of the priest, the Levite, and the Samaritan.

"Rise up, ye women, that are at ease; hear my voice, ye careless daughters; give ear unto my speech." "Enlarge the place of thy tent, and let them stretch forth the curtains of thy habitations: spare not, lengthen thy cords and strengthen thy stakes; . . . Fear not; . . . for thy Maker is thy husband; the Lord of hosts is his name; and thy Redeemer the Holy One of Israel: the God of the whole earth shall he be called. For the Lord hath called thee as a woman forsaken and grieved in spirit."—Isa. 54:2-6. "Behold, thy people in the midst of thee are women."—Neh. 3:13. "Arise and thresh, O daughter of Zion: for I will make thine horn iron, and I will make thy hoofs brass: and thou shalt beat in pieces many people; and I will consecrate their gain unto the Lord, and their substance unto the Lord of the whole earth."—Mic. 4:13. Zion is spoken of as the Church, and her daughters are commanded to arise and thresh together the wheat into the garner and fruit unto life eternal. "Be in pain, and labor to bring forth, O daughter of Zion," for "the kingdom shall come to the daughters of Jerusalem (Mic. 4:8, 10), and thou shalt build the old waste places."

Among those who shared in the publishing of the Word, we find the woman of Samaria, the worth of whose labor alone can be appreciated or told in the day of eternity. We have this interesting and touching story recorded in John, 4 ch. The reader will remember that Christ was a Jew, that is, by birth he descended from the family of Abraham, and belonged to the tribe of Judah. The disciples also were Jews. The Jews, as a nation, had no dealings with the Samaritans. Jesus came, knowing all these things, to "a city of Samaria, which is called Sychar." "Now Jacob's well was there. Jesus, therefore, being wearied with his journey, sat thus on the well [the curbing or wall]; and it was about the sixth hour. Then there cometh a woman of Samaria [or of the city of Sychar] to draw water." Jesus seized the opportunity; the wall of Jacob's well was to him a pulpit; its waters his text. He there preached to that Samaritan woman, and her heart was opened, and, without a doubt, she then and there by faith drank of that "river the streams whereof shall make glad the city of our God." The change wrought in that woman was of such a nature that it affected her after-life to that extent, that nothing more is said of her drawing water from this well. Like the fishermen who left their nets to follow Jesus, she left her water-pot, and went her way into the city, "And saith to the men, Come see a man that told me all things that ever I did: is not this the Christ?" Now we have the woman's text—"the Word was made flesh." You will remember this woman was addressing the men of the city, and Christ was her text. The length of her discourse we cannot give, but we rejoice over the result of the message that fell from the lips of this God-sent messenger. "And many of the Samaritans of that city believed on him [that is on Jesus] for the saying of the woman."—John 4:39. Paul says, "I am not ashamed of the gospel of Christ, for it is the power of God unto salvation unto every one that believeth." So, according to Paul, the saying of the woman proved to be the power of God unto salvation to the people who heard and believed. In this case the Lord's Word did not return unto him void, but did accomplish that whereunto he sent it. Even if it was spoken by a woman, it proved to be a "savor of life unto life" to those who accepted it.

Paul struck the key-note when he said, "Faith cometh by hearing, and hearing by the Word of God."—Rom. 10:11. But again we are confronted with the question, "How shall they hear without a preacher? and how shall they preach except they be sent?" These are important questions, and should have the prayerful attention of the reader. God needs not to be taught of man; his wisdom is infinite; his ways are past finding out, and he is no respecter of persons. He is maker of our bodies, and the Father of our spirits, and "in him we live and move and have our being." He hath said, "Without me ye can do nothing," and also, by the mouth of his inspired apostle, "Covet earnestly the best gifts." We learn that "the gifts and calling of God are without repentance."—Rom. 11:29. Again Paul says, "Desire spiritual gifts;" and James says, "Every good gift and every perfect gift is from above, and cometh down from the Father of lights." And again Paul says, "Stir up the gift of God which is in thee;" that is, cultivate this gift, use the talent that Heaven has bestowed to the honor and glory of God. "Neglect not the gift that is in thee." Surely God has a right to bestow his gifts upon whom he pleaseth, and that women have received a gift to prophesy (preach), none will deny. To tell them they should not use this gift, is like telling a bird it should not use its wings in flying.

"Hath not the potter power over the clay to make such vessels as suit his taste, or such as may be of service to him?" "O house of Israel, can not I do with you as this potter? saith the Lord. Behold, as the clay is in the potter's hand, so are ye in mine hand, O house of Israel."—Jer. 18:6. Even so, has God not the authority to distribute at his own will the talents, requiring them again with usury at our hands?

Then let his work be our pleasure, since Christ hath said, "Follow me." "Enlarge the place of thy tent, and let them stretch forth the curtains of thine habitations," in your efforts to bring the world to Christ. "Spare not;" but rather declare the whole counsel of God, and thereby "lengthen thy cords and strengthen thy stakes;" "for the Lord hath called thee as a woman" (Isa. 54:2, 6) to share in this great work. "Lift up your eyes, and look on the fields; for they are white already to harvest." Many women have passed through that harvest field: and with them precious sheaves have borne away to fill the treasure-house of God. They have toiled, worn and weary, through many a cloudy day, sometimes fainting even by the way. At midday they have toiled, while the sun has in his effulgent beauty shined; in the evening the chilly winds, passing over the field of ripened grain, have fanned their brows. With new energy and faith aroused, across the field they have hurried with sickle in hand. We see in the evening gray the shadows stretching far o'er the lea; the gates are opening to let the gleaners pass; a carriage waits for the sheaves. We hear a call like music ring in the air, and they come with their sheaves in their arms; the sweat is on their brow; their step is light and free. As through the gate they pass, "Good night," we hear them say; "my work is done." We stand alone; the shadows are gathering thick and fast about us: in the stillness of the night we hear the rumbling of wheels amid the sighing of the field; music is on the breeze, and we turn in the direction of the melodies; and lo the reapers, in robes of white, on a chariot ride. We watch them in their flight, and suddenly there comes a flood of light; we see the "city of gold"—"the house not made with hands," "coming down from God out of heaven, prepared as a bride adorned for her husband." And a voice says, "Lift up your heads, O ye gates; and be ye lift up ye everlasting doors." Here, in front of the gate, the grand procession comes to a halt, and shouts of welcome rend the air, while ten thousand times ten thousand angels come out to escort the guests into the King's presence. And we hear a voice saying, "Whose are these, and whence come they?" Lost in wonder while gazing on that spotless throng, one answers, and says, "These are they which came up out of great tribulation, and have washed their robes and made them white in the blood of the Lamb." There is neither male, nor female, neither do they marry any more, but are as the angels of God in heaven. "And a voice said, Alleluia, and the four beasts and the four and twenty elders said, Alleluia; Alleluia; Amen." "This is God's host."

During the ministry of Christ, there followed him many women whose hearts were open to receive his Word, and they ministered unto him of their substance. They were the last at his cross, and first at his tomb. Even from his birth they were engaged in proclaiming his truth. At his presentation in the temple, a woman named Anna spoke of the story of redemption (Luke 2:38), realizing that in him dwelt "all the fullness of the Godhead bodily." Scholars tell us that this is the very same word used with reference to Christ in Mark 2:2: "And he [Christ] preached [spake] the Word unto them." Anna spake of redemption; preached redemption through Christ; spake the Word; preached the Word unto the people. "And how can they preach except they be sent?" By reference to Luke 8:47, we find that Christ constrained a woman to declare his power to heal, for "When the woman saw that she was not hid, she came trembling, and falling down before him, she declared unto him before all the people for what cause she had touched him, and how she was healed." And he bade her "be of good comfort; . . . Go in peace." "Whosoever shall do the will of my Father which is in heaven, the same is my brother, and sister, and mother."

Let us turn again to the woman of Samaria. She was a Gentile, and was regarded as springing from the most depraved and degraded of all nations. In addition to this, she was a woman of impure life; yet to her Christ discourses freely upon the very loftiest of themes; revealing to her more clearly than he ever had done to his disciples, his mission in the world, and the true nature of his spiritual kingdom. It is indeed a remarkable fact, that he made the first proclamation of his Messiahship to this woman. No wonder the disciples marvelled! This conversation was an object-lesson to teach them that the middle wall of partition was to be broken down, and that even the poor Gentile women were to have a share in the privileges and the blessings of his kingdom. After this woman heard his word, she went back to the city, and began her missionary tour, and we know that because of her word many of the Samaritans believed on him. And "so we preach, and so ye believed." Paul says the gospel is "the power of God unto salvation to every one that believeth." The conclusion is that the woman of Samaria preached the gospel; the people who heard it believed her words and were saved.

Again, it is evident that women are to take part in the gospel ministry, for Christ said: "The kingdom of heaven is like leaven, which a woman took and hid in three measures of meal till the whole was leavened." Then, according to Christ's own word, the women are to assist in this work, until the whole, or the masses, are leavened. "Purge out, therefore, the old leaven that ye may be a new lump." This truth is taught in the story of Mary and Martha. Jesus retired often to their house for rest; Mary sat at his feet and heard his word, but Martha was cumbered about much serving (Luke 10:40). All in a worry, she came to the Master and said: "Lord, dost thou not care that my sister hath left me to serve alone? bid her, therefore, that she help me. And Jesus answered, and said unto her: Martha, Martha, thou art careful and troubled about many things: but one thing is needful; and Mary hath chosen that good part, which shall not be taken away from her." Here he administered a well-merited rebuke to Martha, and to all others who would hinder a woman from sitting at the feet of her Master, or from answering the summons: "The Master is come and calleth for thee." There is something for a woman to do besides drudging. For her who heeds His call

"Too short for the service are now the days,
And joyously full of the happiest praise!
Hither and thither the Master sends
His willing servants among His friends,
And all who gladly his tasks pursue,
Find more than enough to hear and do;
Nor has any reason for loneliness
Whom the Master will call, and calling bless.
For joy and restfulness came to me
With "the Master is come, and calleth for thee."

It is evident that sex amounts to nothing in the kingdom of God; for in heaven both are to be "equal unto the angels." A woman poured costliest perfume upon his head, and bathed his feet with her tears, and wiped them with the hair of her head. The highest commendation ever conferred upon mortal was given to this woman.

And Jesus said, "Let her alone; why trouble ye her? she hath wrought a good work on me. She hath done what she could; she is come aforehand to anoint my body to its burying. Verily I say unto you, wheresoever this gospel shall be preached throughout the whole world, this also that she hath done shall be spoken of for a memorial of her." Mark 14:6-9. But how many of our modern preachers have spoken of this in our churches. It is seldom, if ever, heard.

It is John, the beloved disciple,
    Who tells us the story so sweet,
Of Mary who brought the rich ointment,
    And poured it on Christ's blessed feet.

'Tis a tender and beautiful story;
    For she lavished her costliest treasure, With
never a thought of reward,
    Upon Him she loved above measure.

She knew not that in lasting remembrance
    Her name the future should hold;
Nor thought that in gracious memorial
    The tale of her love would be told.

But e'en as she stood by the Master,
    And none but He thought upon her, The
scent of her thrice precious ointment,
    Pervaded the house where they were.

The offering she made unto Jesus,
    But all of the guests in the room
Were told of the honor she paid Him
    By the breath of the fragrant perfume.

And Mary in tenderness bending
    For service, her sole loving care,
In wiping the feet of the Savior,
    Bore the odor away in her hair.

O beautiful type of good doing,
    Sweet symbol of what they may win,
Who give their dearest heart's treasure,
    Thinking only of Jesus therein.

The fragrance of the offering so precious,
    Shall be known in the spice-laden air;
And the head with oil shall be anointed,
    Though that were no part of the care.

This feast was an offering by woman;
    'Twas woman—a pious woman—who first
Gave all her living to her Savior,
    And for you the story is rehearsed.

A poor widow by Christ was commended because she gave her all to his cause. How few of the men have ever done as much! Then, O woman, go your way, let his work your pleasure be; since Jesus calls the woman to himself, saying, "Thou art loosed from thine infirmities," they are free as was the Canaanitish women to present their claims before him.—Matt. 15:21-28. As a Gentile this Syrophenician woman had no claim upon Christ, whom she addressed as the son of David. Here we are again taught that even Gentile women in Christ have a share in the blessings of his kingdom, and are at liberty to serve him. She came to him in behalf of her daughter, and at first "he answered her not a word;" whereupon "His disciples came and besought him, saying, Send her away," thus treating her with cool indifference; but he answered and said, "I am not sent but unto the lost sheep of the house of Israel." Israel was his own; and he was no mere wonder worker; he healed for something beyond and better than the restoration of health and strength. That she might recognize him as her own, he would not, as the disciples suggested, abruptly send her away. So, bowing lowly before him, she repeated her request, saying: "Lord, help me." Whereupon he said: "It is not meet to take the children's bread and to cast it to dogs." It was as much as to say, I am the son of David, I am the healer of Israel, Why should I help you? It is like taking bread from the children [Jews], and giving it to dogs [Gentiles]. And she said: "Truth, Lord: yet the dogs eat of the crumbs which fall from their master's table." She was willing to trust him for all, or to take anything at his hand he saw fit to give—even as a dog willingly takes a crumb thrown from his master's table. Such faith brought the best blessing, and unlocked the storehouse of God: hence, Jesus said unto her: "Be it unto thee even as thou wilt; and her daughter was healed from that very hour." "This was the Lord's doing, and it is marvelous in our eyes."

Again, we learn that "He [Jesus] went throughout every city and village, preaching and showing the glad tidings of the kingdom of God;' and the twelve were with him, and certain women, which had been healed of evil spirits and infirmities, Mary called Magdalene, out of whom went seven devils, and Joanna the wife of Chuza, Herod's steward, and Susanna, and many others," etc.—Luke 8:1-3. These, with the disciples, followed the Savior while on earth; they witnessed the miracles he performed, and from him they received their charge after his resurrection. These women stood near the cross after the Twelve had fled; and they were present at his burial and saw where they laid him (Mark 15:41, 47). They were the first at the sepulcher on the morning of the third day; they were the first to see his face, and to hear his words after his passion: and it is no wonder that they were present at Mt. Olivet to partake of his parting blessing. They obeyed his injunction, "Tarry ye in the city of Jerusalem, until ye be endued with power from on high;" and they were present on the day of Pentecost, and received the promised baptism of power. From this we conclude that Christ conferred upon women the right to officiate in a public way in the service of God.

Both Luke and Paul teach that it is the chief business of an apostle to be a witness, or to testify to the resurrection of Christ. Women were the first commissioned to do this. Moreover, to them he revealed the fact of his ascension, as an event of the near future, and bade them publish these glad tidings to the other disciples. They came and told the disciples, that they had seen the Lord, and that he had spoken these things unto them. We may say what we will, but it remains on record that the apostles themselves first heard the gospel of a risen Lord from the lips of women. We may call women a prophetess, or not, as we like, but to her belongs the distinguished honor of having first proclaimed the principles, or very foundation facts upon which the Christian religion is based, and upon which our hope of heaven depends.

It is an established fact that the women of the apostolic age did preach, and the Scriptures sustain her as a preacher, no matter what women-gaggers may say. These facts stubbornly refuse to adjust themselves to any of their proposed theories. To all who have studied the Bible, and have had no pet theory to support, this truth is as clear as a sunbeam. Unquestionably God has set the seal of his sanction upon the ministrations of women as religious teachers. Any attempt upon the part of any one to hinder her, is but the usurpation of authority, and without Bible proof. But there are some who belong to the class of whom it is said, "Neither will they be persuaded, though one rose from the dead." But God is carrying on his work in spite of these poor, puny adversaries. "If God be for us, who can be against us?"

This forward movement of woman challenges the admiration of the Christian world; and the Church has already recognized her as a prophetess, with a right to teach, provided she will cross the ocean. That means a Christian woman, born and reared on American soil, may preach Christ in India, China, or Japan, but not in her native land. What gross inconsistency! Who can believe that this state of things will long exist? "Tell it not in Gath, publish it not in the streets of Askelon; lest the daughters of the Philistines rejoice; lest the daughters of the uncircumcised triumph." "For the women of my people ye have cast out." "O daughter of my people, gird thee with sackcloth. . . . I have set thee for a tower, and a fortress among my people, that thou mayest know and try their way."—Jer. 6:26, 27. "Who is wise, and he shall understand these things?" for the wise shall understand.

If "the wilderness and the solitary place shall be glad for them, and the desert shall rejoice and blossom as the rose;" it will be to a great extent through the influence of women. And the trend of affairs is leading to the time, when the *proviso* will be struck out, and women will be recognized as teachers and preachers in our home land. He who believes that women have a right to teach in Asia, and not in America, can believe anything. The absurdity of such a position can be seen at a glance. If women have a right to teach and to preach in heathen lands, they have the same right to teach and to preach in their native land. And if they may teach and preach, they should have the same recognition that men have. If she does the work of a minister, she ought to be recognized as a minister.

We believe that women are capable of receiving the impressions of the Holy Spirit—in other words, a call to the ministry. And all must admit that, "We ought to obey God rather than man." The Lord certainly understands his business, and can make known his will to whomsoever he pleaseth. To give a reason why he should not give the evidence of a call to the ministry to a woman, would be no easy undertaking. We think these evidences are just as conclusive and known in the same way, as that of regeneration.

O great and eternal God, Father of our Lord Jesus Christ, Maker of heaven and earth, Creator of all things, Preserver of men and women, Thou who didst vouchsafe to woman the birth of an only begotten Son, Thou who didst say, "And the Holy Ghost shall come upon thee, and the power of the Highest shall overshadow thee."

Come and hush the Church to rest,
As a mother stills her child upon her breast.

As thou didst fill with thy Spirit, Miriam, Deborah, Huldah, Hannah, Ruth, Esther, Anna, Mary, Priscilla, Phebe, and Philip's daughters, and other good and noble women—fill the hearts of the daughters of America with thy love, and with a burning zeal for thy cause; that they may worthily perform the work committed to them. So shall thy name be glorified, our cords lengthened and our stakes strengthened.

Then shall the vision of Zechariah be realized and his prophecy fulfilled: "Then lifted I up mine eyes, and looked, and behold there came out two women, and the wind was in their wings; for they had wings like the wings of a stork: and they lifted up the ephah between the earth and the heaven. Then said I, . . . Whither do these bear the ephah? And he said unto me, To build it an house in the land of Shinar; and it shall be established, and set there upon her own base."—Zec. 5:9-11. In this land of Shinar, which is Babylon, we find the cities of Babel, Erech, Accad, and Calneh (Gen. 10:10). This is the land of idols, and of great wickedness. "Many shall run to and fro, and knowledge shall be increased," and "By his knowledge shall my righteous servant justify many." "He shall bring forth the headstone thereof with shoutings; crying, Grace, grace unto it." These women shall "build it an house in the land of Shinar." "Other foundation can no man lay than that is laid, which is Jesus Christ." Literally, these women have not the wings of a stork, but the work shall be accomplished with such rapidity that comparatively the work will move on as a stork on the wing. As a bird's wings were made to be used in flying, so God bestows gifts upon women, not to be dormant, but to be used in the promotion of his cause. If the prophecy of Zechariah is ever fulfilled, the women must aid in spreading the gospel; and if ever the idolatry of the cities of Babel, Erech, Accad, and Calneh, is overthrown, and their people christianized, it will be through the instrumentality of women: for this is a work that God says they shall do.

"The Lord hath made room for us, and we shall be fruitful in the land." "And they that shall be of thee shall build the old waste places;" "for we are reconciled unto God in one body by the cross, having slain the enmity thereby;" "for through him we both have access by one Spirit unto the Father." "Therefore let your feet be shod with the preparation of the gospel of peace;" so shall the earth yield her increase, and the heavens shall drop with blessings: and righteousness and peace shall kiss each other.

"Therefore, whether it were I or they, so we preach, and so ye believed." "So Christ is preached; and therein I do rejoice, yea and will rejoice." "For we preach not ourselves, but Christ Jesus the Lord, and ourselves your servants for Jesus' sake. For God, who commanded the light to shine out of darkness, hath shined in our hearts, to give the light of the knowledge of the glory of God in the face of Jesus Christ." The ability is of God, and we cannot preach ourselves. We may make an oration, or a flowery speech, and yet this is not preaching. "Without me ye can do nothing," is just as true with regard to preaching as to any other religious work, and unless the minister has been called of God, as was Aaron, and has received the anointing of the Spirit, he or she preaches himself or herself, and not Christ Jesus the Lord. "But we have this treasure [or gift] in earthen vessels, that the excellency of the power may be of God and not of us." "I certify you, brethren, that the gospel which was preached of me is not after man. For I neither received it of man, neither was I taught it, but by the revelation of Jesus Christ."

Who knows for any but himself whether he has been taught of God? We have no right to judge others except as Christ said, "By their fruits ye shall know them." But, if we make this the test, then the decision is in favor of woman; for many of them have gathered much fruit, and the souls by them led to Christ, are numbered already by the thousands. On the other hand, the test will show that some men have answered who were not called. God makes no mistakes. "Whoso readeth let him understand."

### "SHE HATH DONE WHAT SHE COULD."

Do your work and do it well;
Do not stop to think or tell
That the work is small or low.
Do your duty as you go.

Hear your Lord and Master say:
"Go and glean for me to-day;
Gather up the golden grain,
Bring it safe to me again."

Let the reapers far before
Take the finest grain. There's more
Scattered o'er the ground. There'll be
Work enough for you and me.

Then one day, when you shall stand
With your sheaf at His right hand,
Your Master will pronounce it good,
And say, "She hath done what she could."

## BY WHAT AUTHORITY?

———o———

The Church has been brought face to face with this question, and it must be settled soon. Whatever contrariety of opinions may exist concerning woman's sphere, all agree as to her superior moral and religious status. With due deference to one and all, we will proceed to investigate this subject, hoping it will be profitable to the reader, and beneficial to the world.

1. The Presbytery has ever been considered able to decide, who should be received as candidates for the ministry, with a perfect right to license and ordain the same, when in its judgment it saw proper; no other Presbytery, not even the Synod, or the General Assembly, having any voice in the matter. Whoever heard of such a thing as one Presbytery asking another, or even asking the Synod, or the General Assembly, Shall we proceed to set apart to the full work of the ministry, such and such a person? Such a question from any Presbytery, sent to our higher courts, would be treated with contempt, if not hooted at.

2. Each Presbytery has a perfect right to adopt any rule it deems proper; or, in a word, concert measures that in its judgment will aid in the spread of the gospel and the growth of the Church in its bounds. (See Confession of Faith, p. 87, sec. 31.)

3. "To the Law and the Testimony." We, as Cumberland Presbyterians, believe that God has one Church, and but one. Not one in the prophetic age that died, or sank into oblivion, but one Church organized in the family of Abraham, and perpetuated through the "Dark Ages."

So let us stick to the text. But *one* Church—the same in both the prophetic and the apostolic ages—with her ordinances of divine appointment. Christ having abolished death, and having brought life and immortality to light through the gospel, by faith we are made one in him, "and are built upon the foundation of the apostles and prophets, Jesus Christ himself being the chief corner-stone; in whom all the building fitly framed together groweth unto an holy temple in the Lord; in whom ye also are builded together for an habitation of God through the Spirit."—Eph. 2:20-22. Abraham being the father of the faithful, in the Church under the prophetic age there were two sacraments, namely: Circumcision and the Passover. The former pointed to "the circumcision made without hands;" the washing of regeneration and the renewing of the Holy Ghost;" whereas the latter pointed to "Christ our passover." "Purge out therefore the old leaven, that ye may be a new lump, as ye are unleavened. For even Christ, our passover, is sacrificed for us." In the Church, in the apostolic age, we have the same truths symbolized by water baptism, and the sacrament of the Lord's Supper. We have then, as we see, the same Church, and the same truths symbolized by the same ordinances. However, they are different forms of the same ordinances, and not new ordinances and a new Church. So we have one Church with circumcision and the passover under the old, and baptism and the Lord's Supper under the new dispensation. These are but different forms of one and the same sacrament. Let it be remembered that these are sacraments in the Church.

Now the question arises, Who has a right to administer these sacraments? Let us turn to the old statute book. By reference to Ex. 4:25, 26, we find that a woman named Zipporah administered the sacrament of circumcision. Now let us ask, in the name of light and truth, if the Church is the same, has not woman a lawful right to administer the same sacraments now? If not, when and where in the law has it been abrogated? We find by reference to Judges 4:4, A woman named Deborah, a prophetess, was at one time judge over Israel. Now, if she had no lawful right to such a responsible position in the Church, why is it that God has not revealed it to us in his Word of truth? Nowhere can it be found in the Bible that any one person, much less the Church, made any complaint whatever. On the contrary, everything goes to prove that it was no new thing in the Church for a woman to sit as judge, and to look on that people with a prophetic eye. Truly, consistency is a precious jewel, and is of great worth.

Again, Solomon said, "There is nothing new under the sun." We have no doubt but that in his day, and to him, this was true, but it is not true to-day with us. We have new inventions, new laws, new text books, and the Cumberland Presbyterian Church is not asleep to the surroundings. Priding herself in her activity, she rises, and in her strength she creates new boards; and without any authority from the Confession of Faith, the General Assembly proceeds to elect a ruling elder for Moderator. The presbyteries catch the spirit, and fall into line, and ruling elders are considered eligible for the Moderator's chair. This is all brand-new, and, to say the least of it, is without authority, and contrary to the Confession of Faith. But you say, Did it not become a law in our Church when the General Assembly elected an elder as their Moderator? We answer, emphatically, no; for the reason that the General Assembly has no power, nor authority to make law. It may urge, request, receive, and decide all appeals, references, and complaints, regularly brought before it from inferior courts. It may give advice and instruction in conformity with the government of the Church, and in general may recommend to the lower courts measures for the promotion of charity and truth.

As it was when our Confession of Faith was made and revised, even so it is now. The presbyteries alone have the power to make law. (See Confession of Faith, p. 94, sec. 43.) But you ask, Is it not allowable that ruling elders be elected as Moderator? and that, too, by the Confession of Faith, inasmuch as the same section grants the General Assembly the privilege of concerting measures for the promotion of charity, truth, and holiness, throughout all the churches under its care. We answer in the same sense, that it allows the ordination of women to the whole work of the gospel ministry, and in the same sense, it allows women to partake of the Lord's Supper, or to go as missionaries to heathen lands.

Again, by reference to Ex. 15:20, 21, we find that Miriam, the prophetess, the sister of Aaron, had very important charges committed to her care; and there seems to have been considerable responsibility resting upon her, when she went to the lead, as the children of Israel journeyed from Egyptian bondage to the land of Canaan. As a prophetess, with a timbrel in her hand, she shared with Moses and Aaron in that great work to which God had called them, saying, "Bless ye God in the congregations, even the Lord, from the fountain of Israel (Psa. 68:25, 26), for he hath triumphed gloriously; the horse and his rider hath he thrown into the sea." We find the position of Miriam was of such vast importance, that when she became affected with leprosy it became necessary for the children of Israel to camp and wait for her recovery. (See Num. 12:15, 16.) After that, she was received again, and Israel journeyed on. She was as truly called to her position as a leader by God, as was Moses or Aaron. "And the Lord came down in the pillar of the cloud, and stood in the door of the tabernacle, and called Aaron and Miriam, and they both came forth" (Num. 12:5), and received their charge. We learn that Aaron was faithful to discharge his duties as a priest. Can we not truthfully say the same of Miriam? She received her charge from the same source. God called them at one and the same time. "I speak as unto wise men, judge ye what I say." Has any one ever been sent forth by higher power? As a woman, she was faithful to the trust committed to her, and though she be dead, she yet speaketh. "For I brought thee up out of the land of Egypt, and redeemed thee out of the house of servants, and I sent before thee Moses, Aaron, and Miriam."—Mic. 6:4. In this case the question certainly is answered—she received her authority from God.

Again, by reference to I. Sam. 2:1-10, we find that a woman named Hannah spent a great deal of her time in prayer and supplication, and she tarried long in the temple, and the Lord opened her mouth, and loosed her tongue, and while rejoicing in his salvation she said, "There is none holy as the Lord: for there is none beside thee: neither is there any rock like our God. The Lord killeth and maketh alive; he bringeth down to the grave, and bringeth up. He will keep the feet of his saints, and the wicked shall be silent in darkness." If this woman did not preach a good sermon, it was not because she lacked for a text, and the reader will remember that all of this took place in the temple of the Lord, the place of worship. She there warned the people against talking proudly, and speaking vainly, giving them to understand that the living God was he that would weigh their actions, and that the adversaries of the Lord should be broken into pieces, "for the Lord shall judge the ends of the earth." Then let us give her the fruit of her hands, and let her own works praise her in the gates. For God hath said, "Strength and honor are her clothing; and she shall rejoice in time to come."—Prov. 31:25. Since God called these women to preach, and the Scriptures sanction woman as a preacher, it is surely displeasing to God, and even hurtful to his cause, to have her prohibited from proclaiming his Word.

"The Lord God hath spoken, who can but prophesy?"—Amos 3:8. The gift to prophesy is from God, yet some would have us believe that the women have no authority to prophesy, or preach. Paul says, "Every man praying or prophesying, having his head covered, dishonoreth his head. But every woman that prayeth or prophesieth with her head uncovered dishonoreth her head."—I. Cor. 11:4, 5. This is equivalent to saying that when women speak to men to edification, exhortation and comfort, they must have their heads covered; while the men are to have their heads uncovered, or their hair shorn, or shaven. Paul does not even intimate that there is to be a distinction in their work, but only a difference in the dress, or cut of their hair.

"Doth not even nature itself teach you, that, if a man have long hair, it is a shame unto him? But if a woman have long hair, it is a glory to her: for her hair is given her for a covering."-!. Cor. 11:14, 15. According, then, to Paul the women have as much authority as the men. Hence we conclude that men and women were praying and prophesying at that time, or else he predicts what is to come, and so gives instructions as to how they shall dress. If it were wrong for women to pray and prophesy (preach), why did Paul give advice as to how they should appear on such occasions? If he had said, let them stay at home, then there could have been no room for doubt as to what he meant. It would have been just as easy to say, I forbid the women to pray and to prophesy, as to have said, when they pray and prophesy let them have their heads covered. But he would have her, instead of being masculine in appearance, cultivate the gentler graces; that her adorning be that of a meek and quiet spirit, and her "behavior as becometh holiness; not false accusers, not given to much wine, teachers of good things."-Tit. 2:3. We want to emphasize these last words, "teachers of good things." Who will dare, in the face of Paul, to say she shall not teach? Just as well say she shall drink wine, or be a false accuser. Who will have the audacity to contradict Paul's word? Who will draw the line, and say she may come thus far and no farther? Paul put no limit to her teaching. He did not say she may teach her children at home, or a small class at Sunday-school, and then she shall stop. Christ said, "Go teach all nations." Paul said, let the women be "teachers of good things." I am sure the men have no higher authority.

Again, Paul admonishes the church at Corinth, saying: "Follow after charity, and desire spiritual gifts, but rather that ye may prophesy."–I. Cor. 14:1. Now, if there were no women in that church, and Paul was writing to a church of men only, or if he did not include the women, then it follows that women are not even to seek after, or follow after charity. And if she is to follow after charity, then she may, by the authority of Paul, "desire spiritual gifts, but rather that she may prophesy." So we may all "covet earnestly the best gifts," but rather that we may prophesy (preach). The number of God's prophets and prophetesses is great. The prophetic function was never a new thing to the Hebrew mind, nor indeed to any people, even outside the sphere of biblical revelation. Heathendom has ever abounded in men and women who have been recognized as prophets, and we find those who filled the prophetic function, both men and women, even in the sphere of revelation, and that, too, from the beginning. Either Adam or his wife did prophesy, and perhaps both of them. The probabilities are that Eve was the first prophetess, as unto her the promise was made. She certainly understood that in some way, through the promised seed, they were to regain communion with God, that is, what they had lost in the fall. This fact was typified in the shedding of the first blood, (see Gen. 3:21). We presume that he clothed the woman as well as the man. It is more than probable, God having made the promise to the woman, that she spoke often of it, and very soon made it known to her children; for she doubtless accepted from God the information concerning future redemption through the coming Messiah.

Enoch, Noah, Abraham, and Jacob, were prophets of God; and Moses also was a prophet, as well as a leader of the people. But they were no more so than were Miriam, Huldah, Hannah, Anna, and others who served the Church in their God-given places. To the prophets belonged, to a greater or less extent the office of teaching and governing the people, both in spiritual and temporal things. The Priesthood, on account of corrupt practices and neglect of duty, was reduced to a low condition, and the people sank with it. Then was Samuel, whose mother was a prophetess, raised up, and he established the prophetic order, on account of which he came to be regarded as the first of the prophets (see I. Sam. 1, 2 chs). But this does not change the fact that Moses, Aaron, Miriam, and others, were prophets, and were called of God. The prophets were not only a powerful, but a numerous class. We learn that Obadiah concealed one hundred at one time from the wrath of Jezebel, an unknown number having already been cut off by her. Ahab, king of Israel, at one time gathered together four hundred prophets of the Lord, and but a very small number of them wrote anything; while the majority of them, like Elijah and Elisha, Aaron and Miriam, wrote nothing. No one believes that the ministry of these prophets was a failure and without authority; neither do we believe it died when they died.

The office of prophet was not that of simply foretelling future events: indeed, this was but a part of the prophetic office. A prophet was one, whether man or woman, who spoke for another, as his authorized agent or representative, a certain prescribed message. In other words, the office of a prophet was to make known to man God's revealed will concerning him; to make ready a people for the reception of the coming Messiah; to promote and unfold the ways of the kingdom of God; to warn the people of coming judgments; to speak to men to edification, exhortation and comfort. The saying of the apostle reminds us that these things were written for our sakes. "All scripture is given by inspiration of God, and is profitable for doctrine, for reproof, for correction, for instruction in righteousness." That these prophets looked backward and forward, and were no less preachers that prophets is evident. His words had a present meaning and taught then a lesson to those who heard, as they also have a lesson for us who come after—they influence those of our day, and shall influence the future generations. "And these things were not written for their sakes alone, but for ours also." In like manner the preachers of to-day are influencing those around them, and, to a greater or less degree, the future, or rising generation.

Anna was as truly a prophet, or preacher, as was Simeon, and she "departed not from the temple, but served God with fasting and prayers night and day—and spake of him to all of them that looked for redemption in Jerusalem."—Luke 2:37, 38. She being one of God's prophets, she was his recognized agent to bear his message to man. Are we not, as followers of Christ, under obligation to recognize those whom he recognizes? Then there were Priscilla and Aquila, born in Pontus (Acts 18:2, 26) who were among God's prophets, and at whose feet Apollos, being an eloquent man, sat down for instruction, and they taught him "the way of God more perfectly." So here is a woman who taught a man. Besides these, Philip, the evangelist, "had four daughters, virgins, which did prophesy," or preach.

God has declared that he has "appointed prophets to preach of thee at Jerusalem, saying, there is a king in Judah: and now shall it be reported to the king according to these words. Come now, therefore, and let us take counsel together."—Neh. 6:7. The preaching of these prophets that God has appointed is to be about Him who is "God manifest in the flesh"—about Jesus. One of God's appointed prophets was Anna; she preached in the temple at Jerusalem about Jesus, and proclaimed redemption through his name. On the day of Pentecost the prophets whom God had appointed, both men and women, preached through Him remission of sin. From Jerusalem they were to go into Judea, then into Samaria, and thence "unto the uttermost parts of the earth." The command was, "As ye go, preach," and there is no intimation that the women were to be excluded on leaving Jerusalem. These prophets had a message from

God to deliver wherever they went—they were to tell the same story. Paul says, "He that prophesieth, speaketh unto men to edification, exhortation, and comfort;" and again, "He that prophesieth edifieth the Church." Now, take "edification, exhortation and comfort" out of the gospel, or the story of the cross, and what have you left? Nothing, absolutely nothing; for these three elements combined make up the gospel; they are indeed the very heart or core of the gospel. To prophesy, or speak unto men "to edification, exhortation and comfort," is all that any man can do, no matter how eloquent or how learned he may be. This includes all the elements of preaching, and it is a great deal more than many men, to have been ordained to the ministry, have ever been able to do. It is an admitted fact, that many of them fall far below the standard here set forth. They do not edify, they do not comfort, and most they can do is to get up a wrangle. Yet these men are allowed to sit in judgment on women, who, it is admitted, can preach or speak to edification. Is it not true that a sermon without "edification, exhortation and comfort" is worthless? It does not contain the power of God, and is as lifeless as a corpse in the animal world. Then, according to Paul, the four daughters of Philip spoke to "edification and comfort," and Paul in his travels made Philip's house his resting-place. It is really astonishing, if it were wrong for women to preach, that he did not reprove them for such conduct. We might suppose they were excusable on the ground that they had no husbands, and consequently no other way of gaining information; but then they were *prophesying* (teaching), instead of wanting to know anything.

So we find in both the Old and the New Testaments' times, that men and women prophesied, spoke to the people, as the call of God and the occasion required. God saw fit in his wisdom to use women as judges, as leaders, as prophets, and as teachers under "the Law." Where is the authority for taking those privileges from them under the Gospel?" It has been the prevailing opinion that under the New Testament dispensation, their privileges have been enlarged, and their liberties increased. Why this should not be, and why they should not preach, is a thought difficult of conception. It is true that Miriam was not admitted to the priesthood (neither were Moses and Joshua allowed to offer sacrifices), but that she was recognized a leader by Israel, cannot be denied. And no one doubts but that she was faithful in the performance of her duties, and in the work God assigned her. Deborah was called of God to be Israel's fourth judge; her song of praise is still ringing in our ears; it ranks with that of Moses and Miriam; she should be held up before the eyes of the world, and especially of all Bible readers. Surely no one would strike the record of this great woman from the sacred canon.

Huldah was chosen of God to adorn the sacred record, and to expound the law. In fact the whole tenor of the Scriptures proves that it was nothing unusual for a woman to teach the people, and there is not a single word of reproof or prohibition in the Old Testament Scriptures against woman's preaching. So, whatever may be said against her now, it is certain that she did preach and teach under the Law, and even administered the sacrament of Circumcision.

Christ said as much to the women as to the men: "and ye shall be witnesses unto me both in Jerusalem, and in Judea, and in Samaria, and unto the uttermost parts of the earth." In one instance the Savior compelled a woman to testify, and that, too, in the presence of a large audience.—Matt. 9:18, 26. The first instruction in regard to the evangelizing of the world was not given to the apostles alone, or, if so, some of them were women, because they received the promise of the Holy Ghost as well as the men, and when that promise was fulfilled they, too, "were filled with the Holy Ghost and began to speak with other tongues, as the Spirit gave them utterance." The men on that occasion did not make complaint as some of our modern preachers do. Jews were present from all parts of the inhabited world, and if it were not customary for women to preach, it does seem strange that they allowed it on this occasion. If it were wrong under the Jewish law, strange indeed that no rebuke was given. If the authorities had silenced them then, they would certainly be silenced now and forever by that same authority.

It may be that some of those women were numbered with the apostles, since Paul in after days referred to certain women who were of not among the apostles (see Rom. 16 ch). Paul, writing to the church at Rome, says: "Salute Andronicus and Junia, my kinsmen, and my fellow-prisoners, who are of note among the apostles, who also were in Christ before me." This woman (Junia) was either a noted apostle, or was noted for her success in preaching and laboring with and among the apostles, and her work in the ministry was certainly sanctioned by Paul and the other apostles. Let the reader take whichever horn of the dilemma he will, and he admits that this woman labored in the gospel. It is evident that whatever laboring in the gospel means as applied to men, it means the same to women, and whatever apostleship means, it is the same in man and woman. Paul labored, and the women labored, in the gospel; the language is the same: "And I entreat thee also, true yokefellow, to help those women which labored with me in the gospel."—Phil. 4:3. We know that many persons have tried hard to prove that these women did not preach, but that they were deaconesses, and had the care of the poor, acting as sextons of the churches, and looking after the temporal or financial affairs of the churches; but to one who studies the language, these sayings will have no weight. Paul calls these women his fellow-laborers, helpers, and they were evidently engaged in the same kind of work as he. If he preached, they preached; if he did the church scrubbing, they were helping him. But if they were visiting the sick, scrubbing and cleaning churches, it could not be said they were laboring in the gospel. No more so than it can be said of a man who is plowing and sowing and cultivating the soil. A number of preachers and pastors do not confine their labors to the preaching of the gospel, but in addition to this they practice medicine, or cultivate a farm, or are engaged in other employments. When they are thus engaged, are they laboring in the gospel? Who will say, yes. When women are papering and carpeting churches, or polishing stoves, or doing the church cleaning, are they laboring in the gospel? If so, then some very wicked and profane men are our most efficient workers.

"Study to show thyself approved unto God; a workman that needeth not to be ashamed, rightly dividing the Word of truth." "Salute Tryphena and Tryphosa, who labor in the Lord. Salute the beloved Persis, which labored much in the Lord." It seems that these holy women were Paul's assistants in the ministry, and Persis seems to have excelled Tryphena and Tryphosa, for Paul says she "labored much in the Lord." "Greet Priscilla and Aquila, my helpers in Christ Jesus; who have for my life laid down their own necks; unto whom not only I give thanks, but also all the churches of the Gentiles." The reader will notice that Priscilla's name is called before that of her husband, presumably because she was the chief minister; and we learn also that there was a church in their house; of which church it is more than likely she had charge.—Rom. 6:3, 4, 5. "Greet Mary, who bestowed much labor on us" (another woman who bestowed much labor). "Salute Philologus and Julia, Nereus, and his sister" (ver. 15). I commend unto you Phebe, our sister, which is a servant of the church which is at Cenchrea; that ye receive her in the Lord, as becometh saints, and that ye assist her in whatsoever business she hath need of you: for she hath been a succourer of many, and of myself also.''—Rom. 16: 1, 2. Here it seems that Phebe was sent on business as a servant of the church, from Cenchrea to the church at Rome. Of course Paul would not have recommended her if this had been unlawful work for a woman. She certainly went as an officer of the church with the authority to transact business, and by her Paul sent his letter to the church at Rome.

God says, ''Touch not my anointed and do my prophets no harm.'' Surely the tide is upon us, seeing that God had so great an army of women, who by his authority proclaimed his truth, came at his calling, and went at his bidding. And, according to Paul, they have a perfect right to assist in the transaction of business. Clothed with official authority, Phebe visited the church at Rome under the sanction of the apostle, who instructed the church to render her all the assistance she needed. The business committed to her was certainly the work of the Lord, and of course she could not make it known unless she had a right to speak in the church, else such business would not have been intrusted to her. Strange that the apostle should instruct them to assist her in this business, if it were a shame for a woman to speak in the church—since it is a fact that they must hear her (for she must deliver her message before they could possibly understand the nature of that business) in order to give the assistance needed. The conclusion is, that when Phebe visited the church at Rome that she went as a legally authorized delegate or commissioner, to counsel with that body on matters pertaining to the interest of the church. We, as Cumberland Presbyterians, have a form of commission, and it is similar to that used by the apostle in the case of Phebe (see Confession of Faith, 133, secs. 10, 11). And now ''I [Paul] commend unto you Phebe [Smith, Jones, or Henry], which is a servant [pastor] of the church at Cenchrea [Denver]; that ye receive her [him] in the Lord as becometh saints, and that ye assist her [him] in whatsoever business she [he] hath need of you.'' That is, that you give her [him] a place or seat or a voice in the council or Assembly. Given by order of the church at Cenchrea, and signed by Paul, A.D. 60. ''What I have written, I have written.''

## DEBORAH.

A stately woman, firm and strong, was Deborah;
She ruled with wisdom and gave the law.
When Jabin's army was all in array,
She went forth to battle without dismay.

And there followed in her train
A troop of well-armed men.
Her brave heart was filled with grace
And heavenly beauty lit her face.

By this, she said, "I am what I am,"
'Tis God who calls me here to stand;
And if I would be faithful to my trust,
Meet the enemy I must.

While brooding o'er the cruel wrong,
The enemy's tramping steed did run.
And a gloom o'erspread the sky,
While all that night the wind blew high.

In the morning gray a voice rang loud and clear,
"Up, up;" for God hath said "you need not fear."
This is the day that God hath blessed;
And to-morrow we shall have rest.

For earth's deepest wound which we may feel,
There is the balm of Gilead to heal;
Even poisoned weapons cannot harm,
They are powerless 'gainst his mighty arm.

They can wound, but cannot kill;
And they whose darts pursue us still
To slay us, shall perish in their short day;
And "into smoke shall they consume away."

They may think to strike us dead,
But the waves shall ne'er go over our heads.
The strongest bonds Christ soon will break;
With power the prison soon shall shake.

Our limbs with chains shall not long be bound.
The strongest, fastest chain will not long remain.
These, like the enemy before Deborah, shall fall,
And Christ shall rule and reign over all.

Then, in a calmer, clearer day,
When the mists have cleared away,
The banner of peace shall triumphantly wave
"O'er the land of the free, and the home of the
        brave."

# THE OUTLOOK—
## WOMAN'S PROSPECTS BRIGHTENING.
——o——

As the days in their flight pass into the realm of the yesterdays never to return, their duties and issues pass with them, and the tomorrows become to-days, bringing new duties, new opportunities, and new questions to engage the thoughts and energies of men and women. Frequently do we find the stream of the events of to-day colored and tinctured with the live issues of yesterday; because no great thinkers live, whose spirits are imbued with the zeal and the energy of conviction, principle and passion, to enable them to face the issues of to-day, as truth and progress demand that they should be met. In every science of a prosperous nation's education, there is continually being revealed a lack of method. Old principles will not answer in solving the problems of progress. Old rules must be supplemented with new. Yesterday's wants were supplied, or satisfied, with things insufficient for the requirements of to-day. Past blessings fail to satisfy the needs of the present.

Look where we may, and we see these facts manifested, and the word change, change, change, written upon every tablet carved by the hand of God, or wrought out by the skill of man. Many and wonderful changes have taken place in the last century. It has not been long since the common school teacher was measured by his ability to use the switch. If he could "read, write, and cipher" a little, and had a good strong arm, and a voice that implied a will to use that arm—that was sufficient. Literature, art, and science were undreamed-of luxuries, fit only for the student of wealth and leisure. Then the school-room was locked and barred against woman as a teacher, and almost as a pupil. It was not thought advisable that she should be taught even to write, for fear she might do something that would detract from her high calling as daughter, wife or mother. This absurd idea is fast vanishing away and to-day woman stands man's equal, if not his superior, as an educator; and she is not inferior to him in many other avocations of life. She has surmounted already many of the difficulties thrown around her, and has shown to the world her ability to perform well whatever she undertakes. But even now she is sometimes brusquely informed, "We prefer a man teacher. We don't think a woman can control our school." That such is the case, we all know, and it is but the result of old-fogyism.

The women of to-day, with all their advancements, have much to do in order to establish their capacity to work on an equal plane with the man, and still to maintain with gentle dignity the bright lustre of their true womanly nature. It only remains for woman to take hold boldly of the rights of progress, and to guide her destiny to the highest plane of success. This she may do, if she chooses. To accomplish this, it is not enough to be a lady, merely because birth or education has made her nominally one. There is a work for every one to do; and to establish her true dignity and worth, woman must have some noble purpose in life, and work for its attainment. Labor develops true manhood and womanhood, and there is no true dignity without it. The secret of success lies in doing well the little things of life. When these are done, the requirements of to-day are well and nobly met, and we are thereby prepared for the doing of greater things.

That the reader may form some idea of the progress that Chris-tianity is making, and of the great change that has taken place in the last half century, we will remind him, that it has not been fifty years since the first woman was ordained on American soil, and that now there are nearly eight hundred in the work. The first woman ever ordained in America was Miss Antoinette Brown Blackwell. She was born in Henrietta County, N.Y., May 20, 1825, and was ordained Sept. 15, 1853. Now, many women are preparing themselves for the gospel ministry. Thirty-four were in attendance the first term of Mr. Moody's training-school at Northfield, Mass. This school aims to thoroughly equip for active Christian work.

The high rank which woman has taken in all lands and countries, is due to Christianity. As the nations of the earth have become enlightened, she has been admitted to many callings in life which were once closed against her. That we may see how well she has filled her place in various positions of trust and duty, we here introduce some examples:

Fifteen young Hindoo ladies have been admitted to the new female class of the Campbell Medical Schools of Calcutta, and two hundred girls are now being educated in the medical schools of India; and Madras has already supplied six fully qualified female doctors for the northern part of that country.

Miss Catherine T. Simonds has been teaching with great success for fifty years in the Franklin School at Boston.

Maria Mitchell, the celebrated professor of Astronomy at Vassar College, has discovered eight comets. She has received the degree of LL.D. from three different institutions.

There are one hundred and ninety-six women operators in the great operating room of the Western Union Telegraph Company in New York. In this room a husband and a wife are working side by side. They are perfectly matched in skill, but the man gets $15.00 a month more than the woman. Why the difference?

Women have recently been admitted into Greenwich Observatory, and four have joined the staff of the Astronomer Royal. Their duties will require attendance at all hours of the night.

Chicago has recently appointed five women as health inspectors, viz.: Mrs. Byford Leonard, Mrs. Clara M. Doolittle, Mrs. Marie Owens, Mrs. Mary Glennon and Dr. Rachel Hickey. The salary is one thousand dollars each per annum. These women are clothed with police power, and have already accomplished great good in the remedying of abuses.

Miss Marietta Holley, known as "Josiah Allen's Wife," has made herself famous and rich with her pen.

It is said that Miss Isabel Hapgood, the translator of Tolstoi's writings, acquired her knowledge of Russian from a New Testament and a dictionary written in this language. She is now in Russia, gaining a conversational knowledge of this language.

Miss Melinda Rankin, who was a pioneer Protestant missionary to Mexico, died a few months ago at Bloomington, Ills. At the close of the Mexican War, she was teaching school in Mississippi, and her interest in the religious condition of Mexico was aroused by the reports of the soldiers, who returned from that war, concerning the semi-paganism of the Romish Church in that country. She went to Texas as a teacher in 1847; and in the spring of 1852 she started a school for Mexican children at Brownsville, Texas. Bibles were carried over the Rio Grande by the children from this school, and thus a beginning was made in the evangelization of Mexico. At the close of the Civil War, she entered Mexico as a missionary under the auspices of the American and Foreign Christian Union. She often endured great hardships and many trials, and her missionary career is one of the most remarkable of modern times; yet she lived to be more than fourscore years old.

Very recently Miss Lucia Kimball resigned as teacher in the Chicago Public schools, because she was not allowed to read the

Bible to her pupils. Since that time she has become the organizer of the W. C. T. U. Sunday-school department.

Miss Frederika Neilson, a gifted Norwegian actress, determined soon after her conversion to devote her gifts to evangelistic work. She is said to be a great revivalist. America needs some more such changes as that.

Mrs. General Booth, of the Salvation Army, was often spoken of as the best preacher in England, and it is said that at her funeral thirty thousand people knelt in the greatest auditorium of the world, in London.

Mrs. Garrett Anderson, the leading physician in England, makes an income of fifty thousand dollars a year.

The right of women to practice medicine in Canada, has been established by the successful application of Miss Mitchell (a graduate of Queen's University, Kingston), for license. The Provincial Medical Board of Quebec granted the license.

Two ladies have been elected as principals in the public schools of Dayton, O.

Two of the most successful college presidents in Kentucky are women, viz.: Miss Lottie A. Campbell, of Caldwell College, near Danville, and Miss A. M. Hicks, of Clinton College.

The youngest daughter of Mr. Gladstone is principal of a college for young women, near Cambridge, Eng.

The presidency of Wellesley College has been offered to Miss Margaret Evans, of Carleton College, Northfield, Minn., at a salary of five thousand dollars per annum.

The Methodists have lately founded a college for women at North Baltimore, Md. And a training school for deaconesses has just been opened by the Episcopalian Church in New York. Others in Philadelphia, Cleveland and Richmond will follow.

The first building of a Female College at Huntsville, Ala., to be maintained by the Baptists, will be opened Sep. 1, 1891. The building will cost fifty thousand dollars. So we see the various denominations are making preparation to train their women for public work.

It is said that the largest type-writing business in the country is run by a woman—Miss Mary F. Seymour. She also runs a school of stenography and type writing, which school has turned out many hundred graduates.

Mrs. Georgia A. Peck is the managing editor of the *Boston*

*Commonwealth,* and she is the only woman in New England holding a similar position.

Women are State librarians of Indiana, Kentucky, Michigan, Louisiana, Mississippi, and Tennessee.

Miss Mamie Davis, a telegraph operator at Jacksonville, Fla., staid at her post all through the yellow fever epidemic. Brave and true woman!

Miss Olive Buchanan, of St. Louis, is the first woman to hold the office of United States Deputy Marshal.

Mrs. Charlotte M. Yonge, now in her sixty-seventh year, is busy upon her one hundredth and first book, which is a story of the time of Vespasian.

Mrs. Mary A. Livermore recently preached two successive Sundays at the Universalist Church in Washington.

Kansas has eighty-one women who are efficient superintendents of public schools; and there are now 14,365 women commercial travelers in the United States.

Mrs. Douglas, of Atlanta, is the only woman lawyer in Georgia.

Only a short time ago the Iowa Senate was opened with prayer by a woman. It is supposed to be the first time this was ever done.

There are now about four thousand women employed by the Government at Washington.

Miss Susanna Dunkle, of Newton, Mass., has been treasurer of the United States Bank for fifteen years, and handles about five hundred thousand dollars a year.

One of the most efficient postmasters in the country is Mrs. Thompson. She held her position at Louisville, Ky., for thirteen years, at a salary of four thousand dollars per annum.

Mrs. Frances Hodgson Burnett receives $7,500 a year, for editing a children's department for an English-American newspaper syndicate.

Three young women have been licensed as deaconesses in Chicago, under the provisions made for this purpose by the General Conference of the Methodist Church. Bishop Bowman conducted the consecration service, which had been carefully prepared. It included a form of prayer recorded in the "Apostolic Constitutions."

The Woman's Missionary Society of the Methodist Protestant Church collected last year $4,166.77; and the money given by the women of the Presbyterian Church in the United States, for the past sixteen years, amounts to $2,150,000. This represents the entire support of more than two hundred women missionaries; two hundred native Bible-readers; and more than one hundred and fifty schools. Who would hinder such a work?

The Methodist Church has 15,000 women missionaries at work. Their Women's Missionary Societies, which number 320,000 members, have raised $2,520,000. In the 26,000 Sunday-schools and the 22,361 churches of this denomination, a large majority of the workers and members are women. "Speaking of the vote in the Methodist Episcopal Church on the question of the admission of women as members of the General Conference, the *Congregationalist* gives this item of information about the usage of the Congregational churches: 'In our denomination this question is not likely, if raised, to call forth much discussion. For several years, many of our State bodies have included women delegates, and these in some cases have been in the majority. Women's meetings are a prominent feature of some of the State Associations, and in more than one State it is the custom to include them as parts of the Association programme. So far, however, State bodies have not, we believe, sent women as delegates to the National Council.' Women outnumber men in all our Protestant churches, and few of us will say, that they are inferior to men in piety, or good sense, or loyalty and devotion to the cause. It is harder to give a valid or scriptural reason for excluding them from the councils of the Church, than many wise and good men think."

It is really true that about three-fourths of the Christian world are women.

The Rev. Mary C. Jones has had charge of the Church at Spokane Falls, Wash., for two years. She was ordained, without a dissenting voice, in 1882, by the first Baptist Church of Seattle, sitting in council with six or seven ministers, who were in attendance upon the Baptist Association of Puget Sound and British Columbia. So the Baptists have a woman preacher, and they have even ordained her.

The Universalist Church has forty ordained women preachers, and there is now in the country forty-eight National societies of women, with a direct membership of over 500,000. The largest is the Woman's Christian Union, with a membership of 210,000. Then follow the Missionary, Peace, Suffrage, Philanthropic, and Educational organizations. Twelve of these have joined the National Council, formed to unite all the women's societies into one great league. Now a half million of women are banded together for the accomplishment of good. There are 200,000 women in the W. C. T. U.; 135,000 in the King's Daughters; 100,000 in the Women's Relief Corps; and 35,000 in the Eastern Star.

These women are proving themselves men's equals, and they are laboring to rise to higher attainments. As editors, authors, inventors, lawyers, physicians, architects, astronomers, teachers, officers, and preachers, they have already attracted the attention of the world, and have proved their ability to perform well their parts in life's great drama.

When we consider the great progress that woman has made, and when we draw the contrast between women of fifty years ago and women of to-day, we are forced to the conclusion that the foregoing means something; and that women are fast realizing the fact that a large field is opening to them. It is to be hoped that she will cultivate it well; that she will leave no stone unturned. Prophesying daughters will yet be the crowning glory of the Church and of the dispensation ushered in at Pentecost.

We will now take the boldness of Deborah, God's mouth-piece and commander-in-chief, who lead the army of Israel to battle, and to whom God gave the victory; and Miriam, the faithful and called of God; and Huldah, the expounder of the law, who for wisdom, at that time, could not be excelled; and the adoration and thanksgiving of Hannah; and the intercession of Esther; and the piety of Ruth;—and with all these graces blended the Church shall be united, and the world shall be girdled. Then let us take the faith of the Syrophenician woman; the aptness of the woman of Samaria; the humility of Mary; the office of Phebe; the zeal of Priscilla; the gift of Philip's four daughters; the spirit of the woman who gave her two mites; the devotion of the woman that anointed the Savior's feet; the position of the women who labored with Paul in the gospel;—by the union of these excellences of character, the world shall be filled with gladness, and heaven with music.

In order to realize the progress that is being made, and to comprehend what the future has in store for us, it now becomes necessary to give a glance at the past, by considering the position of women but a few years ago. It is a well-known fact that she had but few privileges. Our own mothers tell us that they can remember the first time they ever heard a woman pray in public. But a few years ago, there was no such thing as a woman's prayer-meeting; our Woman's Board was a thing unheard of; the Woman's Temperance Association would have been a fright to some of our grandmothers; our missionary societies were not even dreamed of; and then woman as a teacher to the foreign lands would have been deemed a monster. Women were not considered competent to teach school; they were not even allowed the benefit of a first-class education; and they were not thought of as preachers. We can scarcely realize the rapidity of the change; but he who does not see it is blind to the surroundings. We are not living in the days of flax-breaks, wooden plows and harrows; we are moving forward, onward, and upward. This is an age of progress and improvement, and as Christianity leavens the masses, woman is being elevated; her privileges are being increased, and her opportunities enlarged. "Time and tide wait for no man." It is but a step from the past to the present,—and oh, what a contrast!

Thousands of women are on the stage of action, and they rank, morally and intellectually with our best and noblest men. High schools and colleges in all parts of the country are open to them to-day. We find them in almost every calling of life, and they act well their part. Some of them are numbered among our best mathematicians, physicians, and public speakers; and yet they have not attained to all there is in store for them. Many doors of usefulness are open to them and their facilities are greater now than they have ever been in the history of our Nation. She that wills may rise to eminence and true greatness. It is true that the currents of to-day, on which woman's bark is buoyantly floating, are tinged with yesterday's scum; but the swell of the rising tide of truth and right, is fast lashing the debris of fogyism away, and at the ebb of the tide her banner will triumphantly wave "over the land of the free and the home of the brave."

The Church is moving forward, and Christianity is on her march and nothing can stop her. The blessings that she has bestowed upon womanhood, shall yet be owned by the world and enjoyed by all nations. The sentinels on the walls of Zion are fast awaking from their slumbers, to hear the salutation, "Watchman, what of the night?" Woman, standing on the ground she has won, is ready to shout victory, as the watchman replies, "The morning cometh." The gospel banner is unfurled, and is waving gloriously in the breeze; and who knows but this is the dawning of the morn, when the Church shall come forth "prepared as a bride adorned for her husband," shining as the sun in his strength? Me-thinks the Church above, in

applause, are now ready to strike their golden lyres, while victory
shall flash along our lines, and souls led by the thousands to Christ
(whether led by men or women), shall crowd Zion's gates. They will
send a pulsation of thrilling joy through the highest heavens, which,
reverberating from all sides of the throne in the temple eternal, shall
ring out loud and clear. Rising and swelling anthems of praise shall
reach to creation's farthest bounds, and all the inhabitants of the
Holy City shall catch the hallowed flame, and prolong the joyful
strain. Without one discordant note, the harmonious music shall rise
in softer, sweeter, grander strains, until heaven's high arches shall
ring, and all the world shall be filled with one blessed jubilee. Then let
gratitude fill every heart, and love engross all our powers, for the
prospect of a glorious future.

After a fair investigation of this subject, we arrive at the conclusion, that great moral revolutions are shortly to transpire, and that
good men and women will soon stand side by side in the defense of the
gospel, and of everything that is pure, good, and holy. The walls that
divide Christian men and women in their work will soon crumble into
dust; for God's people are one people. The opposition now so common will be crushed under the hammer of God's word. The great
King, riding in his chariot, stained with blood, whose gigantic wheels
roll in fire, shall pass over these oppositions, and shall grind them to
powder. The Devil shall not always hold sway, but earth's
womanhood being redeemed shall yet arise, and consecrate her
talents and her powers to God. Then let America's women press forward to higher attainments; for, if Christ is ever proclaimed universal
King, it must be done by the united voices of men and women. If we
bury our talent, or refuse to consecrate all our powers to the work
God has given us, he will take away our talent, and confer upon
others the honor of being co-workers with him. The work which God
has assigned us would delight an angel. They would gladly lay down
their harps of gold, and leave the shining retinue of heaven, to bear
the message of mercy to man—to publish the glad tidings of great
joy. God has seen fit to select you and me, and shall we refuse to go?
Shall we be "disobedient unto the heavenly vision?"

That God has wonderfully and powerfully blessed woman in her
work, all agree. Just as well try to pluck the sun from his orbit, as to
stop her in the work which God has assigned her. The Macedonian
cry, "Come over and help us," is sounding in our ears, and many are
heeding the call, and much by woman has already been done.

Through her instrumentality, Religion's gold chain has bound the hearts of many poor heathen to the throne of God; and yet

> "From Greenland's icy mountains,
> From India's coral strand,
> Where Afric's sunny fountains
>   Roll down their golden sand,—
> From many an ancient river,
>  From many a palmy plain,
> They call us to deliver
>   Their lands from Error's chain.
>
> Shall we, whose souls are lighted
>   With wisdom from on high,—
> Shall we, to men benighted,
>   The lamp of life deny?
> Salvation, oh, salvation!
>   The joyful sound proclaim,
> Till earth's remotest nation
>   Has learned Messiah's name."

Women of America, and of God, let us, for the sake of what he has done for us, give ourselves wholly to his work, seeking the guidance of the Holy Spirit, remembering that we are not our own, that we have been bought with a price—even the blood of Christ. The fields are waving with ripened grain. "Thrust in thy sickle and reap: . . . for the harvest of the earth is ripe. Come, get you down; for the press is full, the fats overflow; for their wickedness is great." "Well enough" is never attained. It is impossible to stand still; we must go forward or backward. Which will we do? Oh! who will come to the front? Our motto is, Forward, march. Let us rally, and advancing in God's name, let us look to the hills from whence cometh our help. Let us like Paul "press toward the mark for the prize of the high calling of God in Christ Jesus." Let us willingly give our hearts and our hands to the work which God giveth us to do.

## MY CALL TO THE MINISTRY.

——o——

The author of this little volume was born at Millwood, Grayson County, Ky., March 24, 1862. Her father, Anthony Layman, is still a citizen of that county, and, from her earliest recollection, has been a member of the Baptist Church, and for a great many years has served his church as clerk. Being a man of moderate means and of Baptist faith, he did not take the interest in education that he might and should have done, and being taught from early childhood of Jesus Christ to the exclusion of all others, and that they alone could preach a pure gospel, having the legal right to administer the ordinances of the Church of God, it would be nothing more than natural that to some extent the writer would entertain this opinion. But, thanks be to God, there has been a change. Old things have passed away and all things have become new. When but a child, in my twelfth year, I was led by the Spirit to seek the atoning merits of Christ's blood. When all was laid upon his altar, it pleased God to accept the offering, pardon past offenses, and save from sin and guilt the unworthy caller for his name's sake. Thus peace was made with God, being sealed with the Spirit of promise, and I was made to rejoice in God my salvation. Soon after, I was impressed to labor in the vineyard of the Lord, seeing the harvest was truly plenteous and the laborers few. But feeling my inabilities, I was made to inquire, who is sufficient for these things? In this I found no relief and felt to excuse myself on the ground that I was too young. Not having so much as ever heard of a lady preacher, and knowing that there would be opposition, I tried to persuade myself that it was not right for women to preach. I was uneducated and many obstacles were in the way; and to say the least of it, the struggle was a hard one. Thus I passed my girlhood days.

On February 20th, 1879, I was married to Curtis G. Woosley, of Caneyville, Ky. I entered upon the duties of a wife with a light heart, hoping to find relief by getting my husband to respond in my behalf. This I failed to do. I would gladly have the hand laid on him that I felt was laid on me. Instead of getting rid of the impressions, they were made more sensible. In order to justify myself in refusing to obey the instructions of the Holy Spirit and go to work for the Master, I set to work to read the Bible through carefully, marking all the places where a woman was mentioned. From these notes I have written this book, and now send it out, as I hope, to bless the world. I pray that it may help others to decide to work for the Master.

In the fall of 1882, I began my Bible search on this question. I commenced with Genesis, and in the summer of 1883 I found myself at the *Amen* of Revelation. I was now convinced of the fact that God, being no respecter of persons, had not overlooked the women, but that he had a great work for them to do. My impressions were felt more sensibly than ever before. I felt, "Woe is unto me if I preach not the gospel." In my search for relief from the Bible, instead of finding any comfort, I found sorrow of heart. A dark cloud overspread my sky; the light that once shone across my path was gone; and my hope for heaven was at times almost cut off. I now began to doubt my conversion; I felt I had made a mistake. During this time the darkness increased; the storm beat hard against me. Thus months passed, and I was so miserable, that my life was a burden, and I did not care to live: and yet my way was not clear—I was afraid to die. I prayed: "O Lord, restore unto me the joy of thy salvation," and promised to work for him if he would only restore and bless me as at first. The blessing came so full that I could not doubt his forgiving love.

Then I felt to say: "The people will not hear me, and I cannot get any work to do, and my husband will not be willing to let me go." So I excused myself, but the conviction still followed me—my duty was as clear as a sunbeam, and I saw and understood it just as clearly as when I came to Christ a poor penitent sinner. I saw in him a fullness and felt my sins forgiven; but I said: "How can I go? my people will dislike it." Here language fails me, and none but those who have been called by God to leave their homes and friends, and labor in the vineyard of the Lord, can know anything about such a struggle. The painter's brush could not paint the picture, and none but God and those whom he calls can understand it. We cannot tell it, but like the man born blind whose eyes Jesus opened, I can only say, "One thing I know, that, whereas I was blind, now I see," and "herein is a marvellous thing;" I know two things, the one as clearly as the other: namely, that God for Christ's sake has forgiven my sins, and that he has laid his hand upon me. But I kept this locked up in my own heart. "Neither told I any man what my God had put in my heart to do."

By this time other difficulties were in the way. It pleased God to bless our marriage with two children—a sweet little girl and bright little boy. Now I excused myself by saying, I cannot leave my children; they need my care and attention, and with them I must and will stay. None but those who have experienced the dealing of God with mortals, know anything of the darkness and gloom by which I was surrounded. Still I refused to heed the motor within. But God knew best, and he doeth all things well. The hand of affliction was laid upon my firstborn, a sweet little girl. I was stricken with anguish as the physician said, Your child is beyond the hope of recovery. Heart broken, I went to my closet and besought God for my child. I felt that God was opening the way and intended to remove the hinderances, though it be by death. I laid myself and child upon his altar, saying, "Thy will, O God, be done. If thou wilt have me preach thy gospel, give me back my child. By this may I know and thy work I will do." It pleased that God, who worketh when and where he pleaseth, to spare my child. Truly God works in a mysterious way his wonders to perform, and his ways are past finding out.

I found upon recovery of my child that I was still unwilling to go. I said, "Now I am slow of speech, I am not educated, and the people will not hear me. And perhaps my husband will not be willing." But God did not excuse me. My promise was continually before me. Oh, how dark those days! My health now began to fail me. In the fall of '85 I found myself confined to my room; six months later I was reduced to a frame, and as helpless as an infant. My promises stood out before me. I had so often promised and then refused to obey God, it seemed like mockery to make another. So I hesitated. My duty was made plain to me. I was impressed if I would consent to preach my health would be restored, and the strength needed should be given. Thanks be to God! I have found it even so. And I now rejoice that through God I overcame the weakness that flesh is heir to, and that by his grace I would stand for God and preach the gospel. Sink or swim, live or die, his work henceforth should my pleasure be, and to win souls to Christ should be second to nothing. As I write, I bless God for that day and the victory gained. Though unable to raise myself in bed, I laid myself, my husband and two dear children upon God's altar, and with all my heart I said, "Oh Lord, lead me in a plain path, and show me thy way, that I may walk therein." By faith I put my hand in his, as he reached out to help me, and thus far he has led me even all the way. And now with Paul I can say, "An effectual door has been opened unto me, and woe is me if I preach not his gospel," for "I have opened my mouth unto the Lord, and I dare not go back."

My health began (soon after giving all to God) to improve. I made known to no person my intention to preach the gospel, being fully determined to improve the first opportunity afforded. On the night of Jan. 1, 1887, I found the way open. I was called upon by the session to conduct the services of the hour, our pastor not being present. At first I thought to excuse myself, but before I could do this my promises rushed in upon me, and I said, By the help of God I will do the best I can. And for the first time in life I went to the sacred desk and opened my mouth for God, Oh, that was a precious hour—a green spot in my memory. A happy season it seemed. My sun had reached its meridian height, and the light of the Lord in its effulgent fullness shone round about me. My sky was without a cloud, so happy was I in the discharge of duty. I felt that the days of darkness were past, and that God's approval rested upon my labors. But, alas! this state of things did not last long. The fire of opposition began to burn. A cloud arose, and the winds of adversity began to blow, and the waves of criticism beat against me. Friends of former days were now foes. Even my father turned his back upon me. All earthly help failed me, and so I don't wonder that no man taketh this honor to himself, but he that is called of God as was Aaron. The storms may rage, the winds may blow, the waves may roll high, but I never expect them to go over my head. And through them all thus far I have been safely led. To-day, my sky is clear, the storm has abated, and my God on the waves is walking; the winds he holds in his hands, his voice like music I hear as it falls in accents so sweet on my soul, saying, "Peace, be still. Fear not, for I am with thee." And in the light of this new day, after a year's hard struggle and toil in trying, amid it all, to hold up Christ as the sinner's friend and the Savior of men, what could give us more joy than to look out and see a father coming back to meet and own his child! To-day I thank God that he has given me back my father and my friends, and counted me worthy to suffer for his name's sake. And I rejoice to know that I go forth with the good wishes of all my people.

In the fall of '87 I was received by the Nolin Presbytery as a candidate for the ministry. In November, '88, I was licensed to preach the gospel. In November, '89, I was ordained by said Presbytery to the full work of the gospel ministry. I have been since that time trying to win souls to Christ, by leading them from darkness to light, from death unto life. I have endeavored to sow the seed in the morning. God being my helper, I expect to bear the heat and the burden of the day, and in the evening withhold not my hand. Let me ask you, dear reader, for your prayers, that I may be able to gather fruit unto life eternal, that God may be glorified in the salvation of many souls. When I first started in this work there were but few houses open to me. Now I have calls coming from every quarter. For all which I give God the glory, for he is worthy. A bright future is before me, yet I know not what awaits me. But through God I expect to conquer. With Paul I can say, "As much as in me is, I am now ready to preach the gospel to others, glorying not save in the cross of Christ, by which the world is crucified unto me and I unto the world. From henceforth let no man trouble me, for I bear in my body the marks of the Lord Jesus. Therefore, I testify unto you that in all ages they that fear God and work righteousness are accepted with him. For with God there is no respect of persons, neither male nor female in Christ.

As said above, upon my sick bed I decided to go to work for my Master. I made a full and complete sacrifice of myself and my all. I gave my husband and children to the Lord, and trusted him alone for everything. Since that time I have not counted anything as my own, but as the Lord's. At that time I had only one little home, but now God has given me thousands of friends, who have opened their hearts and their homes to me. When I first entered the field, we were greatly in debt, on account of sickness, and we had no money. I did not stop for that, I went right on, and made arrangements for meetings, even without a cent of money to pay my traveling expenses. The means have always been provided, and my needs supplied, sometimes in an almost miraculous way. And I thank God that to-day I owe no one anything, but to do him good and to help him on the way to heaven. In this sense, I feel that "I am debtor both to the Greeks, and to the Barbarians; both to the wise and the unwise. So as much as in me is I am ready to preach the gospel" to others; "for necessity is laid upon me."

I have now been in the work four years, and thank God for the day I started. I commenced my work in humble places. The first summer I preached out-of-doors, in the open air, and in school-houses, but God blessed my labors. On account of opposition in my own denomination, we have failed to get some valuable members. At one time, at the close of one of my meetings, the Methodist Church received forty additions. At first I had no calls scarcely at all from my own people, but now they come from every quarter, and it is impossible for me to respond to one-tenth of the calls I receive. I can say truly God has opened for me an effectual door.

During the four years of my ministry I have preached nine hundred and twelve sermons; for which God has given me two souls each. For two thousand souls more I am willing to consecrate the remainder of my life to God. Over five hundred have been received into the C.P. Church under my ministry. With a joyful heart, and a bright future before me, I lay aside my pen to resume the duties that God has made obligatory upon me. Let come what may, I know the Lord God and the Holy Spirit have sent me.

"Thus far the Lord hath led me on."

"Land ahead! its fruits are waving
O'er the hills of fadeless green,
And the living water laving
Shores, where heavenly forms are seen.

Rocks and storms I'll fear no more,
When on that eternal shore;
Drop the anchor! furl the sail!
I am safe within the vail."

I have learned by experience that, "All that will live godly shall suffer persecution." But we have the promise of the life that now is, and of that which is to come. When our glorious work is done, and time on earth is passed, and eternity is begun, and God has gathered us up into his house of "many mansions;" amid the chiming of the towers of the great city, and the songs of welcome, we will press our way up to the throne, and lay our trophies down—all down at Jesus' feet. And then on golden harps we will join in singing praises to his name.

www.ingramcontent.com/pod-product-compliance
Lightning Source LLC
Chambersburg PA
CBHW031537040426
42445CB00010B/586